M.A.R.E.S.—Mature, Attractive, Respectable, Even-Tempered, Single, Professional Ladies Over Forty - Captivating Younger Men -

Move Over Cougars.
There's a Real Lady in Town

M.A.R.E.S.——Mature, Attractive, Respectable, Even-Tempered, Single, Professional Ladies Over Forty - Captivating Younger Men -

Move Over Cougars.
There's a Real Lady in Town

SHERRY LYNNE

M.A.R.E.S.—MATURE, ATTRACTIVE, RESPECTABLE, EVEN-TEMPERED, SINGLE, PROFESSIONAL LADIES OVER FORTY - CAPTIVATING YOUNGER MEN - MOVE OVER COUGARS. THERE'S A REAL LADY IN TOWN

iUniverse books may be ordered through booksellers or by contacting:

iUniverse
1663 Liberty Drive
Bloomington, IN 47403
www.iuniverse.com
1-800-Authors (1-800-288-4677)

Because of the dynamic nature of the Internet, any web addresses or links contained in this book may have changed since publication and may no longer be valid. The views expressed in this work are solely those of the author and do not necessarily reflect the views of the publisher, and the publisher hereby disclaims any responsibility for them.

Any people depicted in stock imagery provided by Thinkstock are models, and such images are being used for illustrative purposes only.
Certain stock imagery © Thinkstock.

ISBN: 978-1-5320-1098-9 (sc)
ISBN: 978-1-5320-1097-2 (e)

Library of Congress Control Number: 2016921388

Print information available on the last page.

iUniverse rev. date: 02/15/2017

DEDICATION

M.A.R.E.S. is dedicated to all the single,
professional, ladies who are ready to
experience love in a positive, meaningful,
manner they have never experienced before,
regardless of the age of your mate.

TABLE OF CONTENTS

LIST OF ILLUSTRATIONS

FOREWORD

Many write books from a researcher's perspective. They have not experienced the subject matter in which they write. There are copious amounts of statistics, evidence, numbers and case studies. M.A.R.E.S. is not that type of book, nor is it a textbook filled with examples of excellent grammar and punctuation. It is a fun and enlightening read about the body, mind and spirit of M.A.R.E.S. in relationships with younger men.

However, for all of you hungry minds, a small amount of research will be shared because it is fulfilling to some to delve into the topic, and be able to play around with numbers and facts. As a past university Instructor of English Composition for 6 years, I always expected my students to back up their essays with research and citations. Here, I will do the same.

The meatiest part of the book comes from personal experiences. No amount of research, fact-finding, statistics, case studies or the like can impart what personal experience can offer. I have earned two Bachelor of Arts degrees and a Master of Arts degree. I have instructed, lectured, coached, and trained in plentitude, academically and practically for over twenty-something years. Nothing has prepared me professionally and skillfully as much as life. Nothing has taught me more than experiencing life first hand.

An Author friend of mine mentioned, when I was concluding this book, I should speak about those in the LGBT community who see themselves somewhere in my classifications of M.A.R.E.S. It is definitely not my intent to leave anyone out. Truth is I do not know enough about the community and how it classifies members. My goal for this book is not to present a ton of research. It is written from a perspective of what I know, what others I know, know, and personal experiences. We will see what my next endeavor brings. By then, I SHOULD be able to write something about that community which is truthful and on point.

ACKNOWLEDGMENTS

have kept this book close to my chest like a poker player holds her/his cards. The few who knew about this book have been in full support of it. They are listed here. The order does not determine how much they have given. I am truly thankful for all who have been my cheerleaders and pep squad members, I needed the positive energy They have inspired me, motivated me, phoned or text messaged me in the early and late hours of the day; given me research information, let me use their apartment as a hideout and even gotten others I don't know in on it. Some have been driven to assist with this project because of its relevance today.

I could not have done this without them. Some are:

- My mother, Rosetta J. Fairmon who took many calls of progression of this book and told me I had to finish it.
- My "unique" dad, John H. Moore, Sr., - need I say more

- My brothers and sister - Steven L. Moore - for ALWAYS checking up on his little sister and discussing sports as a break from this project. John H. Moore Jr. (JJ) and Darlita Moore-Thompson - prayer warriors and future "road dogs"
- Cousins - Lisa, Beth, Carla, Desiree, Matthew - too many to name
- My best friend, author, and coach in this effort -Kathy Hopzapfel (Pen names: Lauren Bach and Cate Noble- please buy her novels. She is an incredible writer of romantic suspense)
- Incredible supporters - Justin Rosenbaum, Carol Pillow, Julie Bragg, Dr. Audrey Wilson-Allison (Professor), Pamela K. Roberts and Dr. Kathleen Weber, MD. -Smooches
- A new bff, mom, wife, and sister author from California too - who writes paranormal horror (buy her books too!) - Carol J. Marshall
- And the many friends who loaned stories, cheered me on, and continued to motivate me.

And to God, the Creator of everything, including this book, THANK YOU for the vision, the words, the inspiration to keep going, causing unbelievable things to me to suddenly work out, and for all YOU are to me.

Thank you all from the top,
and bottom, of my heart.
-ml (much love)

DEFINITIONS

Developing man – younger man

Forty-plus – women or lady over forty

Forty-something – women or lady over forty

MARE/M.A.R.E.– abbreviated version of M.A.R.E.S. Sometimes it fits better

Stallion – younger man; more distinguished man

Cougar – The grammatically correct way of spelling this term is "cougar." I spell it was a large "C." When some think the word, it can be interchanged with some women's name. To some, it is also a brand.

INTRODUCTION

The term "Cougar," and I'm not talking about the mountain lion, is used to describe women over forty who pursue relationships with younger men. (I will use the words developing men, younger men, or stallion interchangeably since the name of the book is M.A.R.E.S./MARE) Please remember this. In some instances this is true, but at other times there is a misunderstanding as some women are not the ones to be in hot pursuit of a man. The man is in pursuit many times, of the more stable, secure, attractive and experienced women.

From what I read and hear, Cougars are women over forty who go out to bars and clubs looking for the stallion to have fun with; only wanting a very temporary relationship. They are deemed to have no morals and would leave their "hunting ground" with whoever is left at the establishment. The movie, "The Graduate," used to be the calling card for the old terminology, "the May-December" relationship in which the woman is much older than the man, and is shunned.

In my opinion, many "Real Cougar" women and according to Linda Franklin author of "Don't

Ever Call me Ma'am: The Real Cougar Handbook" are now out to dismantle this perverted and antiquated way of thinking. Television shows like "Sex and the City, Desperate Housewives, and Cougar Town" in conjunction with real life actors and other professional women are here to demonstrate the real Cougar is a confident, attractive, fun loving, and financially secure woman who attracts a man searching for those qualities. These men want women who are secure, with more life experience, and with no "drama."

I have discovered indeed some women are real Cougars, and for them it is a good thing. However, I know there also exists another class of ladies who belong to an elite, exclusive group. I have coined the acronym M.A.R.E.S. to represent this group. M.A.R.E.S. are Mature, Attractive, Respectable, Experienced and Even-Tempered, Single, Professional, Extraordinary ladies. Not anyone can be a M.A.R.E. Why not? And how did you come up with this name?

When I started to write this book, I was inspired by a younger, male friend at the job I had. A few years ago, he told me he was befriending a woman and she was a Cougar, forty something as I was; yet she was single. I was married at the time and let's just come to an understanding; married women should not be preying on young, single guys. When I thought about being called a Cougar, I had to mull over what definition he was referring to. I knew it was a compliment because it had come from him, a friend, but what did he mean? There were many definitions swimming around in my head, both positive and negative. I was confused. Did he mean Cougar because of the age difference between us? Did he mean Cougar because he thought I was "on the prowl" for a stallion? Did he mean Cougar because of the maturity, attractiveness, independence and youthfulness he saw in me that attracted developing men? Or was it something else? Hmmm...

For research and for general information, I continue to visit Internet sites on dating and some more specific sites on Cougar dating. Many of the blogs by men and women on Cougar dating, commend the more experienced women who find attraction and love in younger, developing men. Other sites have negative comments about women who find attraction, bonding and love with these men, and are pretty malicious. Still others ask why some have to place a label like "Cougar, sugar mamas etc." on these women. Labels, labels, labels. They ask, "Why can't they just be women attracted to men? Why stipulate age?" Many of them also comment on how mature men have been with younger women since the beginning of time so why can't a more established woman be with a developing man? BRAVO!

I have a personal answer to the question about labeling; yet have no sound answer for why some cannot accept the age difference. For years, people have categorized/labeled not just things like designer clothing, luxury cars; suburban living versus urban living, but it has always categorized people as well. Black, white, rich, poor, celebrity, blue collar, white collar, professional, working class and the list goes on and on. I figure if some people are going to label something or more specifically someone, then why not be the first to come up with a positive label? Unfortunately, words/titles/labels whatever you want to call them carry some weight and can have a bearing on someone's self-esteem or confidence.

This is why I came up with the term M.A.R.E.S. A mare, the horse, is experienced, beautiful, graceful, a protector, and strong, possessing oodles of character. I thought this new category of ladies fit this title.

Why did you spend your money to purchase this book out of all of the other books you could have bought? I believe most people relate to personal stories. I know I do. It can be your own personal experience or experiences from others you know. In this book, I share knowledge and insights I have personally gained in my own life, not what some researcher takes notes on, or a study they have conducted on strangers. This is active, real involvement and exposure to events or people in my life, whether in the present or in the past.

Now don't get me wrong, research and second hand knowledge is not to be dismissed. I had to do research to earn all of my degrees. Where the rubber meets the road is I want to read about people who are like me; women who have had some of the same situations happen to them. I want to learn first-hand how they deal with, and how they feel about what is happening to them. From my perspective, one cannot receive feelings and advice from research. It takes being in someone's shoes to understand what they are going through which makes matters relatable.

So, grab your favorite beverage and snack, and walk with me as I share my experiences with you. This is an easy read. You will not need a dictionary or have to put on your thinking cap to read this. Feel your way through this and find what speaks to you in what you read. Remember, I am not an expert with a bunch of degrees in relationship psychology, sociology, or the like. I am simply someone who has gone through a different school we call personal experiences and/or hard knocks. My education from life has taught me valuable lessons and continues to enrich my years in many ways.

As you continue on your own journey, (for those who see themselves as a M.A.R.E.S.) please look at what I share as learning opportunities or affirmations. If you are not a MARE, but know someone who is, then this should lend understanding to you about those who might be in the same situation as me. It might be your mom, aunt, cousin or even a friend who is a M.A.R.E.S. and attracts younger men. I have and I continue to experience these learning opportunities and they will too.

"Go after your fairytales, they
are not just for kids."

CHAPTER ONE

Creation of M.A.R.E.S.

When I was seven years old, my dad took my two brothers and me horseback riding for the first time. It was a frightening experience because the animal to me seemed massive. "Why didn't they start me off on a little pony?" I wondered.

As I stood on the ground, looking up in awe at my horse, I heard my dad tell the stable people, "Give me the roughest one you've got," and I cringed. They showed me how to mount the horse and told me she was a seven-year-old mare who used to race. I was instructed to pet her and give her some apple before mounting her, then we'd become quick friends and she would take care of me.

I had to admit she was a beautiful, shiny and graceful horse unlike the steed my dad was mounting who was unable to keep still and, was attempting to remove the bit from his mouth. The horse did not want to be controlled, nor did my dad want something to control him. It was an interesting battle between two, prideful males.

Sherry Lynne

Searching for an appropriate title and animal names to describe this new and special league of ladies, that experience came to mind.

Fox, pig, rat, swans, stallions, studs, snake, ugly ducklings, cougars, chicken, bitches (It is a real word and in the dictionary with its Old English, origin before the 12th Century; used to describe female dogs then, but has other meaning now!) were in use, describing certain groupings of animals, in conjunction with describing characteristics of humans.

Awakened at 5:01AM on a Saturday morning, the name mare came to me. Eureka! I thought about the character of the female horse I had ridden many years ago and knew this was it!

A mare is said to be a mature horse as she is over 3 or 4 years of age, but still able to bear foals and take on her younger counterpart, the filly. The mare is easier to handle than a steed (as I witnessed when I was seven!). She is said to be more intelligent and courageous and will work harder for her owners. She's loyal, yet can be territorial. If she is a lead or boss mare, she takes charge of her herd, and her leadership comforts them. The herd is known to rest easier and longer, trusting she is protecting them. Finally, mares are winners. They have won Kentucky Derby's, the Preakness, the Belmont Stakes, and the Melbourne Cup; Zenyatta won the 2009 Breeders' Cup Classic. Astonishing for a mature lady.

Creation of M.A.R.E.S.

What Makes A Woman a M.A.R.E.S.?

In my decision to call this new class of ladies mares, I developed the acronym M.A.R.E.S. to fully describe who these ladies are, and their character traits. M.A.R.E.S. are:

<u>M</u>ATURE/MELLOW - She looks at life's experiences as lessons learned. She has become skilled at not seeing failures as negative, but views them as hurdles to jump over. Get it? She is secure and confident because life has taught her to be this way. Life is not centered on her. She knows this, therefore is not a drama queen.

<u>A</u>TTRACTIVE -She is attractive not just on the outside, but on the inside as well. She is striking and good-looking, deserving of a second glance. She is appealing and very interesting in conversation. She draws a person in because of her intelligence and modesty. She definitely has the "wow" factor, and any man regardless of his age, is attracted to her. This characteristic is especially mesmerizing to a developing man I am told because he gets his physical AND intellectual needs met by her.

<u>R</u>ESPECTABLE- She is highly regarded and has gained admiration for her contributions at work, home, in the community, with family, friends, and those who know her. She has a good reputation. She earns respect and gives it as well. Honor and decorum are her middle names because this is how she is known. She is the epitome of class.

$\underline{E}$XPERIENCED AND $\underline{E}$VEN-TEMPERED – She has been either exposed to or involved in many learning opportunities in/of life. The M.A.R.E. has an understanding and awareness of her surroundings and can adapt to them. Mild mannered, low maintenance, and mellow are other words describing the M.A.R.E. She possesses many emotions, but knows how to keep them in control.

SINGLE, PROFESSIONAL, EXTRAORDINARY LADY – She is and has true friends. She is devoted to them and connects with them because of her emotional stability and secure aura. She is a loyal and trustworthy friend to all she includes in her circle and she is faithful to them and to herself. A M.A.R.E. has learned to balance her career and her social life since both are equally important to her.

According to Franklin, Real Cougars can be married, my M.A.R.E.S. on the contrary, are single ladies only. She one day hopes to be married. Her goal is to find her own, special someone. The M.A.R.E.S. does not purposefully set out to find a developing man. She is merely seeking a man to share her life with and desires to find love. She has no age in mind, only compatibility, happiness, and fulfillment. If he happens to be younger than her, then good for them. Her relationship with a younger, developing, single man is not a "Mrs. Robinson" relationship. It is deep and it is as serious as the two involved want it to be. If she's happy and he's happy, then no one or nothing else matters.

As you can see, M.A.R.E.S. are very special ladies and not ones to be taken lightly. I know you're thinking, "Who in the world can fit this description?" They are a rare group. The holiday commercial where Santa Claus meets the M&M candy, they see each and both faint is grand example of how one feels when they meet a M.A.R.E. Both echo, "They do exist!" (One of my all time favorite commercials!) It's a challenging class of ladies to become a part of, but I am doing my best to stay in this association. It takes character building, everyday, to remain in this circle.

You ask, so who are some famous M.A.R.E.S. you know or have heard of? I wish I could tell you I personally know some of the famous ladies who are often mentioned and how their lives follow the pattern of a M.A.R.E. Some who quickly come to mind are: Julianne Moore and Bart Freundlich (about a 9 year difference in age), Deborra-Lee Furness and Hugh Jackman (16 year difference), Shakira and Gerard Pique (10 year difference) Geena Davis and Reza Jarrahy (15 year difference) Gabrielle Union and Dwayne Wade (10 year difference). All of these are approximate age differences. Speaking with and knowing them personally can only confirm these numbers as fact or not. Nonetheless, they offer some insight into age gap relationships. These couples are the ones who have been successful in their relationships, and are together. They appear to know how to work on any issues they have, and manage to keep their personal lives out of the limelight. This makes them respectable, smart and worthy of mention.

From history, the first wife of Prophet Muhammad, Khadijah, was forty years young when she married him. He was 25. She was said to be beautiful, came from a prominent family, and was a wealthy businesswoman. He, contrarily, had little means, was her employee, was credited to be a great caretaker and protector, and proved to be an astute businessman with her affairs. She was captivated and impressed by him thus vowed to marry him even though there were 15 years separating them. It is said they had "the most loving, happiest, and sacred marriage of all human story."[i]

"Wait for it..."

CHAPTER TWO

Becoming a M.A.R.E.S.

had been married to my ex-husband for years. We met my sophomore of college and became immediate friends. You know how it is when you meet someone you instantly like as a person? He had a girlfriend and I had a boyfriend, and we had respect for each other's significant other. (I was a M.A.R.E. in training and didn't know it.) We occasionally met in the cafeteria, and occasionally went to a basketball game or two. I never thought of him in any other way except as a friend. I had met his roommate and his roommate's girlfriend freshman year and we were friends as well.

At the time, I had been with my boyfriend back home in Chicago since 8th grade, but in my junior year in college. I felt I needed a break in the relationship. I had become a member of a sorority my freshman year and my ex felt I was spending too much time with my sorority. I felt smothered and stifled and thought he was being a bit over-protective of me with other guys. I had been honest, loyal, and in love with him before I went to high school as a preteen.

He had forgotten I was the one who went after him because I was so in love. Ha! What does a 13 year old know about love? Anyway, after breaking up with my ex-boyfriend for a while, I was without a man for the first time since I was 13.

My boyfriend and I reunited my senior year in college. The year I was focused on completing college by any means necessary. In order to do this, I went into seclusion. I became inactive with my sorority, and moved into a different sorority house on campus. I vowed to hide out from 'Greekdom' while working diligently to raise my GPA, and focus on my relationship with my boyfriend.

The sisters of a sorority I had no affiliation, welcomed me with open arms and embraced me. We were from different ethnic and cultural backgrounds, but none of us allowed it to hinder our relationships. Besides for most of my life, I had family members who were also of different racial, ethnic and cultural backgrounds so I felt right at home. I was grateful they allowed me to live with them, and I wanted to get to know as many of them as possible.

At the time, my boyfriend and I still struggled in our relationship. I mean it was a little better, but not good. He asked me to move to the city where he was going to school. I declined.

Still seeing my friend from time to time, I finished my coursework that semester and had some time to just hang out. I asked my friend if he would like to go to a basketball game together. We went and had a great time, not just because our team won, but also because my friend was fun to be around and easy to talk to. When the semester ended, I moved back home awaiting graduation at the end of the next semester. I stayed in contact with him while he finished his coursework.

My friend and I began to talk more and I even went back to visit, under the pretense there were still some loose ends to tie up for graduation. I mailed my friend cookies and thank you cards for his assistance with some last minute documentation I needed to culminate my tenure as an undergraduate. Somewhere between paper work and cookie baking, I began to look at my friend as more than a friend.

When I returned home, my boyfriend and I verbally clashed most of the time. One day in a phone discussion, he did something, which was not in character for him. He was employed at a national fast food restaurant and had decided not to finish his college degree. I was severely disappointed in his decision, and knew it was because of the crowd he had befriended. During the conversation, he swore at me. I always told myself if any man disrespected or abused me physically or verbally, then he would not have the opportunity to do it again. It would be the first and last time it would ever happen. Living up to my promise, I broke up with him.

We both suffered a great deal of emotional hurt and pain because we had been together for long time. We were supposed to be together forever. Get married. Have children. Grow old together, oh well. I received several calls from his dad begging me to go back to his son.

I had become a part of the family and they missed me. I missed them too, but had to stick with my decision.

For support and understanding, I turned to my friend from college because he listened. As time passed, he and I became closer and closer. I started to visit him where he moved after we both graduated. Somewhere down the line, me in my infinite wisdom, decided to pack up and move to the city where my friend lived. Following my heart and not my head, I moved 300 miles from home where I knew no one, except him.

I rented my own place after I arrived and found employment. Starting to miss home, I thought about returning. I mentioned this to my friend. Shortly after my "tales of woe," he asked me to marry him. I responded only after a couple of days of contemplation with the answer of yes.

I knew it was best if I delivered the news of my engagement to my ex-boyfriend in person, therefore I went home to tell him. It was one of the most hurtful pieces of news I had at that point, to give someone. There were questions, tears, and silence on both parts. Leaving the crime scene, I felt like the biggest insensitive, jerk in the world, but I had to move on with my life and he wasn't a part of it.

It's funny, at the same time five hours away, my fiancé's ex-girlfriend showed up at his door begging him not to go through with his plans to marry me. The attempts were futile on both parts. We were determined to go through with our nuptials and in seven short months, we were married. Twenty-four years later, we divorced.

Becoming a M.A.R.E.S.

Let's just cut to the chase. Why are we divorced now, years later? Thank God it had nothing to do with adultery. My perspective is a shared. 50-50 percent, we both were guilty. One, we were too young and my love with and for my ex-boyfriend did not have enough time to properly dissipate before my marriage, my 50 percent. The responsibility my ex-husband needs to except is too much risk taking in business ventures, places a huge financial strain on a marriage, causing it to eventually crumble, his 50 percent.

Why did I give you the background above? The reason I consider myself a M.A.R.E. is because I have experiences and growth the challenges, which have been in front of me. Experiences and many hurdles such as deaths of family and friends, medical conditions, break ups, job loss, and job searching for months in New York City are a part of life. I have lived in five states, moved 12 times, and left close relationships only to start over again in a new city and build new relationships. My past consists of bumps in my financial credit, living on limited income, borrowing money from my parents (several times), experiencing bankruptcy, gaining weight, losing weight, worrying, being stressed, and being in and out of love. The love thing is huge in itself, right? Only to recently become separated and then divorced!

My God holds my hand in all situations. He promises to never leave me or forsake me, and He has been true to His promise. I look back at the cloud of smoke from all of life's adventures and stand in awe as I move through the dust storm. Years ago, driving home from college, a five-hour drive, I hit a dust storm across the flat plains in the Midwest. When I get home, my car is dirty, I'm dirty, and I even have particles of dust in my mouth and nose I could crunch down on. Yuck! I race to the shower and wash from head to toe, then feverishly brush my teeth, floss and rinse with a half bottle of mouthwash.

This is how I feel when I take a long look back at my life. I want the dirt/negativity gone so I eagerly wash my mind for clarity and marvel at how far God has brought me and what He has taught me. I stand now as someone who can relate to many who must travel and have traveled through their own journey and adventure. There are scars, but I now look at them just as a soldier looks at his or her stripes. My stripes are earned through my own personal war and are a sign of being victorious. I know the battle is not yet over. Life will continue to teach me valuable lessons.

I continue to mature because of what I experience and learn. I am beginning (and have a long way to go still) to believe I am attractive on the inside and outside. I believe my character is one worthy of respect as I strive to live a wholesome and fun life. Because of my experiences, I have learned to be even-tempered. Even my students tell me how cool I am and you know how un-cool they can make you. And finally, I work hard at being a special, extraordinary and a valued member of my community. I am loyal and trustworthy to my family and friends. My goal is to get along with other women to best of my ability and as a true MARE would do.

All of these characteristics listed above, which I continue to work on daily, give me the ability to call myself a MARE. In addition to the character aspects of being a MARE, I have been told my persona and appearance has changed significantly. Having nothing to do with my marital status, I lost 30 lbs. How did I do it? One morning I woke up and said, "I'm tired of not being the person I can be physically." I started to exercise five times a week and managed to eat what I wanted but with portion control. Now when some see me, they say I look like a college student. On campus, faculty, staff and students have mistaken me as a student. I have been asked out on dates by younger male students, have had male students call me beautiful (Who me? Seriously is what I honestly think) and tell me how attracted they are to me. (Females as well) I have had faculty and staff fascinated by me and have had female students jealous of me. This is outrageous and has never, ever happened before. My youngest admirer was 18!

Please believe, I say this not to brag because all of it makes me very, very uncomfortable. I share this as a testament to how hard I work at being a lady, a MARE. Seeing and hearing these results are a bit awkward for me, yet they reassure me I am on the right path in my transformation of being a better and more confident person.

Sherry Lynne

It's not easy being a MARE. M.A.R.E.S. are
ladies, refined women. There are times when
M.A.R.E.S. are tested. There are times when we
fail to remain in character because someone or
something pushes too far. The beauty of a lady
such as a MARE is they immediately bounce back
by learning from the challenge, and then moving
on. She knows she is not perfect, far from it.
She is honest enough to know even with daily
practice and refinement of her character, she
will never be without flaws.

"WHICH ONE ARE YOU?"

CHAPTER THREE

Cougars or M.A.R.E.S.
Who's Who? Which One Are You?

The reason I decided to write this book is because I really disliked being called a Cougar. Why? The association of a woman over forty who is in a relationship with a developing/younger man is not common, yet. Some, in society, are not fans of seeing a mature woman with a younger man. They have their reasons why this partnering is unnatural to them.

Cougars are perceived to be a woman who is forty - sixty, even older these days. Most often she has colored her hair to hide the gray, dresses provocatively, and only favors younger men. She is a hunter, a ravenous predator of young, twenty to thirty something, gorgeous men who are in places where Cougars frequent. She sets her sights on her target, then pouncing. This sounds like Animal Kingdom video, yet this is how some in society believe Cougar women to act.

Some think of seeing their mom or even grandma with a younger man perhaps their age or younger, is wretched. Some think mature women should be with men close to their own age. Some think women forty plus with younger men are desperate. How do they define desperate? And some younger, less mature women feel older, mature women are a threat because they are stealing their possible mates.

In 1967, the film "The Graduate" is released. The main character, Mrs. Robinson, is an unhappily, married, alcoholic who meets a young, college graduate at a party given by his parents. Without spoiling the movie, just in case you want to view it, let me state that this older woman's seduction makes for an intriguing and entangling web for this unsuspecting, young man.

For those who fancy being referred to as a Cougar, I must admit this is not the best movie to reveal who a Cougar is. Although Mrs. Robinson, to some, represents the genesis of fictional, Cougar-like characteristics. I would hope today's Cougars would say she is not the poster child for their lifestyle.

In my opinion, if and only if you have watched this movie, you may have reasons NOT to embrace the Cougar lifestyle for your friend or family member. The movie's representation of an older woman/younger man relationship is deplorable. On the contrary, Cougars might state there are very few relationships of this magnitude. Even so, mature women dating younger men are here. Society needs to get used to it.

Looks Are Deceiving

My first day of instruction in August of 2009 at the collegiate level, I was anxious, yet excited. This was my first time instructing at a University. "Was my syllabus and class schedule comprehensive? Were the students going to respect me in spite of my youthful and petite appearance? Had I prepared enough?" All of these thoughts ran through my mind. "Pull it together Sherry! You are well prepared and very capable of delivering the objectives for this course. Now go." I took one deep breath, and approached the podium.

I remember 30 pair of eyes looking at me as I stood there about to take attendance. Making eye contact with each student, one young man stared back. He raised his hand before I could call the first name on my list. He emphatically asked, "You're our professor?" Smiling back at him, "Yes I am." He then turned to another student who must have been a friend, "Man, I don't like English, but I think I'm gone like this class!" Other students nodded in agreement while other students were not yet convinced this is where they wanted to be.

I had one student who stuck out from the rest. He was a football player, white, and a non-traditional student meaning he was over 24. He sat in the third row with his hoodie covering his head I, however, asked him to remove it in order to see him fully. I could tell by his posturing he was the new kid on the block, so was I. We immediately made a connection, so I thought, and in my infinite, professor-type, wisdom, I assured him he would be treated somewhat like the rest of the students. My youthful look may have said one thing, but the command I had over the class said another.

During the semester, the student who initially inferred he was pleased about my façade, soon found out I was tough and no nonsense. Jovial and effervescent, yes. Push over, no way.

The non-traditional student performed well in my class. His writing went from C level to almost an A. He came to my office a couple times for pointers on how to improve, and he did just that. We became friends outside of class and found we had some things in common. I liked football. He played football. I was married. He had been married before. My husband and I were putting the final touches on restoring our historic home, and guess what? He was a contractor.

The next semester, I was teaching a Public Speaking course. When he found out he needed the course, he enrolled in my section. I also had another student to enroll in my course. It was the same student I had in my English class who I found out, was enamored with me.

On several occasions, the enamored student concluded I was giving too much attention to the student who I had befriended. Thinking there was something going on between the non-traditional student and me, he became enraged right in the middle of class. I interrupted my instruction, and asked him to step outside of the classroom into the hall. We spoke of his behavior. I told him it was unacceptable, not befitting of a scholar. He apologized and admitted to his error. Without warning, believe it or not, he asked me out on a date. Being a couple steps ahead of his response, I told him I do not date my students even though he was 19 years young and considered an adult. The other student admitted they had conflict before. He now knew why. He surmised jealousy was the problem and smirked.

<hr />

Who Are Cougars?

I tell this story to assist in understanding the difference between a Cougar and a MARE. Valerie Gibson's book, "Cougar- A Guide for Older Women Dating Younger Men," defines how Cougars came into being and whom they have morphed into today:

> "Edwardian cougars took the "tasty bait" approach. They lay around pale, alluring, and interesting while young swains fed them passionate poems. Then they pounced.

> Times of war were particularly plentiful. While the older men marched off to serve, cougars did their part by devoting their attention to an eager generation of pups only too willing to "serve" in a different capacity.

Despite the sexual revolution in the 60's and 70's, when everything that moved was considered fair game, older women who dated younger men were still taboo. This made cougars growl with frustration. When the female liberation and power surge days of the 80's and 90's arrived, cougars were released from the societal cage. It didn't take long for them to make full and powerful use for their new freedom.

The new, free cougar is a unique breed. She is single, older, and often divorced (at least once). She may have come out of a marriage with a hefty share of the spoils and find that she suddenly has more time (and money) to spend on herself and life's special pleasures, such as drinking, carousing, and spending hours making love...She isn't interested in marriage or in having anymore children. In fact, she often prefers not to share her den. Sexually hot to trot. She is brimming with confidence and allure- that almost intangible aura that is immediately picked up by the antennae of men who know a fascinating woman when they see one...Whatever her situation, what the cougar wants at this point in her social and emotional life just

happens to match up with what many
young men want—hot, satisfying sex
with someone who won't be a lifetime
or live-in partner. It doesn't hurt
if this someone is a pleasure to
look at, fun to be with, interesting
to talk to, and good for the ego.
Someone who can handle more than
one martini without falling over is
an asset too. If she can't get any
of that, plenty of steamy sex will
do very well." (Gibson 16-18)

Well, there you have it. This comes from a
woman who considers herself to be a pioneer
Cougar. At the time her book was published,
Gibson was a Sex and Relationship columnist
for the Toronto Sun. As a radio and television
guest, she was an advocate for older women
dating younger men. Having had five, yes five
husbands, she conceded this fact had made her
have many years of "dedicated research." Might
I also add at the time of her book's printing,
the last husband was purported to be 14 years
younger than she.

There are many women like Gibson, who think
this way. They love life and choose to live it in
this manner. However, there are some Real Cougar
women, according to Franklin, who dislikes
the negative connotation of the title, Cougar,
and is in opposition with Gibson's Cougars.
Franklin's Cougars desire companionship and a
deep, loving relationship with their younger
mates. Hence, there are two schools of thought
by two different Cougar women. Gibson offers

the playful, non-committal, and is accepting of a young man's station in life, school of thought; or Franklin's school of thought, which believes the younger man NEEDS to be confident and stable, bringing three different types of independence to the table. They need to be as emotional, spiritual, and financially independent as the Real Cougar woman. Indeed! Why do these women write about being Cougars from two different perspectives? I offer my reason why below.

The Women's Liberation Movement

Women's rights have been a challenge for over 100 years. The role of women was one of submissiveness to a man. They did not work outside of the home and were only expected to be subservient to men. Women's jobs, at that time, were to get married, birth babies, nurture and raise those babies and be homemakers.

In 1792, Mary Wollstonecraft showed herself to be one of the first feminists when she wrote *A Vindication of Rights of Women,* which purported to be about the moral and social equality of men and women. Doing further research, I found 1848 was the year when the women's rights to vote movement first started. The Nineteenth Amendment to the Constitution of the United States was ratified (approved) on August 18, 1920. It prohibited any U.S. citizen from being denied the right to vote on the basis of sex. This is said to be the "first wave" of feminism.

Cougars or M.A.R.E.S. Who's Who? Which One Are You?

Learning further about the WLM (Women's Liberation Movement), here are some dates worthy of sharing:

- 1949 - Simone de Beauvoir's book, "The Second Sex" is published. The term "women's liberation" is used for the first time. - Yay!
- 1960 - The FDA approves birth control pills. - What???
- 1961 - Eleanor Roosevelt chairs President's (Kennedy) Commission on the Status of Women. - Glad he recognized the need.
- 1963 - Equal Pay Act Amended prohibiting sex-based wage discrimination. - That's right. We work the same. Pay the same!
- The Civil Rights Act of 1964 is passed. It prohibits discrimination in the workplace based on gender. - Women are capable too!
- 1965 - Equal Employment Opportunity Commission is appointed to oversee enforcement of the Civil Rights Act. - What a pity!
- 1966 - 28 women form the National Organization for Women (NOW) because the EEOC fails to enforce of the Civil Rights Act. - Wonder why?
- 1968 - One hundred women protest the Miss America Pageant because it promotes "physical attractiveness and charm as the primary measure of a woman's worth." - Please...
- 1972 - Equal Rights Amendment passes. - Victory for women!

- 1973 - Decision written to legalize first trimester abortions - Roe v. Wade
- 1974 - March for Life. Pro-life rally against abortion in D.C.
- 1975 - Joanne Little acquitted on murder. Precedence set for victim's right of self-defense in sexual assault cases. - And rightly so![ii]

These facts are interesting tidbits of information. This helps to demonstrate how women were viewed in the past compared to where we are today. It's no wonder we are freer thinking and acting today, than we were able to be in the past. Our foremothers leave us a legacy of their struggles in hopes we would safeguard the path they have paved.

Why did the WLM come about? As we know, men have always dominated society. Men and women agree on this. Equality for women is long-suffering. Men have resisted it for a long time, and in some regards, the resistance of equality in some areas is warranted. Physically, women are not giving all of the bodily tools to promote strength as men have been given. Agreed? Yet, men and women have been given equal measures of mental strength. At times, I believe women have been given a little bit more.

Power, whether mental or physical, over something or someone is considered to be one of the greatest weapons of all. When men make decisions for the greater good, the decisions they make, blankets everyone and everything. During the time of the WLM, women wanted rights to make their own selections. I suppose men saw this as lessening their power, especially over a species/women, who were already deemed subservient. If women receive equal rights, we grow stronger. If we grow stronger, then society as a whole gets better. We have all heard the phrase, "A chain is only as strong as its weakest link." Women becoming stronger make men more powerful. But some don't see it this way.

Recently, a movie, *Hidden Figures*, came out which depicts how three black women were instrumental in the Space Race mission. If you have not had a chance to view the film, I encourage to. If not for women's intelligence, then John Glenn could not have been the first, American Astronaut to orbit the earth. Women assisting in scientific and mathematical formulas lend him power to achieve a historical event and become well known.

Nevertheless, there exists no earthy reason why women are/were deprived of equal rights to many things. Conversely today, we look at a women's equal right to date whoever she wants to date. She should be afforded the chance at companionship, love, security, and all she is seeking in a man.

⸻ ⚙ ⸻

So...who first used the word "cougar" and associated it with women who prefer younger men? I am convinced it was men or a women, and here is why:

Men are used to being in charge. They have been in power since the beginning of our creation, sanctioned by the Creator. I have no issues with this. However, in a male/female relationship, they are usually the ones leading, they feel they have more experience, have more wealth, and usually are the oldest. For these reasons, if a female such as a Cougar becomes the initiator to a man, she takes on the role of a man. Men feel they are the initiators in everything. To them, men are created to be in charge and the "hunter" as seen in caveman times to businesses of today. Most men do not want to relinquish such power to women.

Another reason I feel men created the term Cougar is because it describes an animal, which is said to have tendencies to hunt, pounce, then kill its prey. Possibly in jest, a man or two, thought they were being funny when they compared women's behavior with younger men to a mountain lion acting out the hunt, pounce, and kill traits for survival.

If one really considers a man's other reason for calling a woman a Cougar, it is because they are jealous. Lets face it. If an older man sees a beautiful, smart, sexy, and financially sound older woman with a younger man, they are threatened. The younger man is handsome, fit, flirty, focused on his prize, and exudes sexiness; and the older man is or possibly not sexy? Can you say the green-eyed monster has reared its ugly head? Jealousy makes him call her Cougar simply because he is comparing her to an animal.

On the other hand, permit me to postulate the term Cougar could have come from other women. And you know women...

Those women could be younger, the same age as a Cougar, or older than the Cougar. The term could have come out of jealousy, fun, or both. Maybe women in the same age bracket cannot attract younger men, or maybe the women are younger and like the older men, feel threatened by the Cougar. The difference from men and younger women feeling threatened is younger women emphatically state Cougar women are stealing men in their twenties or thirties away from them. For fun, maybe the term Cougar is meant to be a light-hearted way to appreciate a women's choice to date whoever she wants. Maybe another women said in a joking manner to another women, "You are acting just like a cougar. You look for a younger man, then pounce on him." The other woman in a teasing way might have responded, "Yeah. I am hunting for prey. Some young man to devour." Then they start to laugh.

Who knows the origin? My take on it is that there are three choices of who called the Cougar, a cougar first. Men did, Women did, or perhaps both.

Surveying some Cougar friends of mine, about ten, and gathering Intel on the ways of the Cougar, these things came to the forefront. Now remember, these are the actual results of the women who were surveyed. Names have been withheld so I would not look at them "differently" when I saw them. For their privacy, I did not want to know who was doing what:

1. Cougars have rules.
2. Cougars have specific "hunting grounds."
3. Cougars have Do's and Don'ts

4. Cougars have certain categories in describing younger men.
5. Cougars have little inhibitions when it comes to sex.

Number One: Cougars have rules:

A. They are focused when they are hunting. Cougars know exactly who and what they are searching for.

B. They DO NOT travel in packs. No man wants to be scrutinized by a bunch of chatty women. They may hunt alone allow or with a wing person.

3. They don't listen to negative people who tell them dating younger men is a bad idea.

D. Initially to them, age is not important, however they must be at least 18.

5. They must feel, look, and dress sexy. There is competition from Pumas (younger women)

F. For them, it's about the moment. They are not thinking long-term.

G. No sex on the first meeting. They wait until the moment is right.

H. If that moment is that evening...nothing else to be said.

I. They ignore stares, looks, and words from others.

J. They don't take their man home to meet the family, especially kids if they are still at home.

These are the top ten rules. Others are mentioned, but these are the ones most had in common. Cougars of this survey heavily rely on these unwritten rules, but to me what is astonishing is the women did not know each other and come from various areas in the country, yet their responses to the questions are similar. Is it a learned behavior they have studied, or is it simply a coincidence?

In my estimation, it could possibly be both. More than likely, what works for the individual Cougar may be shared with others, Cougar or not. I believe there is no perfect recipe. They see what is effective, and this is what they do. Makes sense to me.

Number Two: Cougars have specific hunting grounds.

Conferences, workshops, auto mechanics garages, bars, night clubs, health clubs, work elevators, parties, electronic stores, ski lodges, everywhere you are able to find a young, single man a Cougar is there.

However, here are (50) fifty the M.A.R.E.S. also considers:

1. Lunch at a popular deli where business people go
2. Coffee or tea at a café. Read a book or newspaper there
3. Assist with a local charity. Animal and Children's are great.

4. Go to Chamber of Commerce luncheons - Sherry Lynne
5. Teach a workshop which caters to men
6. Browse home improvement stores like Lowe's, Home Depot, Ace
7. Shop at Eddie Bauer, Bass Pro Shop, or gadget stores
8. Take the dog for a walk or to the doggie park
9. Learn to play golf and have lunch at a golf course
10. Play on a co-ed sports team
11. Attend a local sporting event
12. Go to a bar for Monday/Thursday Night football
13. Food shop on a weekend or evening
14. Indulge in a free concert or play
15. Don't overlook your service provider. Hint. Hint.
16. Listen to an outdoor jazz concert
17. Find a jogging, walking, or cycling path
18. Take a First Aid or CPR class
19. Register and volunteer at the local Medical Centers
20. Take a weekend singles' cruise or other trip
21. Frequent a pub with a fun, bartender and ask about singles
22. Visit bookstores - Good one!
23. Browse for CDs or a man, haha! at a music store - Sherry Lynne
24. Go to Best Buy and look around
25. Go to art gallery openings
26. Grace with your presence at a car show

27. Get invited to someone's Christmas, New Years, or whatever parties
28. Go to a Super Bowl party
29. Meet with co-workers for Happy Hour
30. Throw your own seasonal party
31. Have lunch at the hospital cafeteria
32. Visit a boating or trade show
33. Shop in a gourmet, wine, or health food store
34. Attend a wine or beer tasting if you can.
35. Take a cooking class for singles
36. Volunteer for a political event
37. Take part in petition, signing drive – go with a group for safety
38. A reunion
39. Go to a different city and take a tour
40. Throw a single, adults, only Halloween party - Sherry Lynne
41. Join a booster club at your favorite college
42. Try an online dating service, if you dare
43. Go to a golf or tennis tournament
44. Attend a civic meeting on key issues
45. Have your car washed on a busy weekend
46. Have good friend set you up on a blind date
47. Take a how to repair something class
48. Have breakfast, lunch, or dinner at a busy sidewalk café
49. Stroll down your local downtown on a weekend
50. Go to an investment seminar. Prepare for your future.

Number Three: Cougars Have Do's and Don'ts – Different from Rules

According to Gibson, the below is a list of the do's and don't of Cougars. She says, Young men are not attracted to these things so Cougar women:

1. Do not fuss, whine, complain, or nag.
2. Do not discuss aches, pains, illnesses or surgery.
3. Do not refuse to drive in a convertible.
4. Do not drink and drive. That's what cabs are for.
5. Do not ever say:
   - Commitment
   - Retirement
   - When I was younger...
   - I'm too old
   - Not tonight
   - Was it good for you?
   - When will I see you again?
   - I love you
   - Is this too short?
   - Is this too tight?
   - Is this too low?

What do good Cougars do?

1. They have a career
2. Know how to be classy at all times
3. They know how to flirt
4. Know how to hold their stomachs in for hours at a time
5. They know how to handle menopause

6. They own vibrators
7. Carry condoms
8. They always smell wonderful
9. They keep fit
10. Maintain a healthy diet
11. They dress to kill
12. Care about how they look
13. Will embrace all kinds of anti-aging techniques to look their best
14. They are financially sound
15. They know how to have fun.

If you want to know more about the Cougar lifestyle according Gibson, I suggest you pick up a copy of her book, and books written by others to explore more detailed information on Cougars. I did.

Did You Decide?

Cougars or MARES? This, for some, is still the question. How do I know which one I am? Attitude and behavior should answer the question. If you find yourself "stalking preying, hunting, pouncing, and on the prowl," you are a Cougar. If you, generally, are making the moves, prefer short-term romps with your prey, and do not desire to meet his friends or family, particularly his mother, then more than likely you have more Cougar tendencies than M.A.R.E.S.

"SOME PEOPLE GROW OLDER, YET
OTHERS GROW WISER."

CHAPTER FOUR

Mature/Mellow

M.A.R.E.S. believe and hold to using her challenges as learning opportunities. Each obstacle in her life she uses to develop her character. In comparison to a maturing bottle of wine, she continues to ripen, getting enjoyable and bolder by the day. When the time is just right, her special man harvests her. He is ready for a lady emotionally and physically mature. To him, she is his fine, artisan wine, flavorful and complete. She is no longer considered immature, but has been refined. A MARE is blessed with the gift of wisdom, which only comes from the lessons she has garnered in life. She is mature and has left juvenile characteristics behind, and refuses to respond to those who make negative comments about her.

While doing research to assist in writing this book, some comments online written by several women under thirty are distasteful. These women write about their impressions of Cougar women. Some women display immature attitudes of jealousy, irrational feelings, and unkindness. They are envious women. Like spoiled, insecure children whose toys are being taken away, these women are whining and complaining about younger men falling for mature women instead of demonstrating grown-up characteristics, and wishing any aged woman happiness and success with a man of any age. This is the reason I have been told developing men find more established women attractive and irresistible. We are more confident and do not play foolish games.

--------------⟡--------------

About four years ago, I met a man who worked for me on a project. I had never met him before, but he was hired to maintain my property. When I went out to introduce myself to him, he just stared at me. At first I thought I had something on my face or my clothing was not in order. He was looking at me so intently; I had to ask if something was wrong. Finally he said, "no." After walking around the premises and giving a little instruction, he began to compliment me on the house. A few moments later, his compliments were directed at me. I don't remember his exact words, but I do remember his continued stares and flirtatiousness, which I simply said thank you to and went back into the house.

When I saw him the next time, I was doing some planting outside.

"Do you like the job we're doing for you?" He asked. "Is there anything special you need us to do?

They had done a great job and nothing more was needed so I said,

"No."

"Are you on Facebook?" he asked.

"Yes I am." I said.

"If I befriended you, would you respond and be my friend? I had longer hair in some of my pictures on there. Let me know what you think. I'm thinking about letting it grow back?"

"Of course and okay."

"Awesome!" he responded. "I'm gonna do it on my phone as soon as I get to the truck!"

"Okay."

Later in the evening I checked my Facebook page. Sure enough there he was with a friend request and a message. After hitting the confirm button, I checked his message. It read:

"Hey beautiful!"

What was I to say except something like?

"Hey back and thank you for the compliment. I told you I would become your friend, which I don't normally do if I don't really know you. Your hair looks good long as well"

"Thank you for befriending me. I have a crush on you, but you already know that!"

I responded back by saying:

"Awww thanks for making me smile!" (What else was I supposed to say?)

"You are so welcome!" was his reply.

Why am I sharing this with his permission? Because M.A.R.E.S. do not go after developing men. We are simply going about our usual day and things like this happen. We become magnets to men without any direct effort. Why? We exude confidence, gentleness, strength, attractiveness and fun, naturally. It is a learned behavior to act like a lady and to respect and treat other's the way we want to be treated. Guys in general are attracted to this. We are not the prowling, pouncing, sex starved women some have accused us of being (Now there may come a time or two or three, after we have won the hearts of our gentlemen where we may morph into this for fun!), but again M.A.R.E.S. do not behave this way to attract a man. The men come to us.

The Way to His Heart

M.A.R.E.S. become skilled at knowing the way to a gentleman's heart is not through what she does for him. She knows buying him things, always being available for him, cooking and cleaning for him and even sex is not the way to bond with a man. Even being intellectually stimulating i.e. knowing recent public events, what's happening in the world of finances, what's going on in the political arena, even the latest technological advancements does not ensure a man's heart. He might love you and find pleasure being with you, but he doesn't feel emotionally connected. A man must feel like he is willing to let himself go and fall in love not just love a woman.

M.A.R.E.S. also know sex does not mean the same thing to a man as it does to a woman. Ah ha. Here's a challenging topic to talk about. S-E-X. Women become attached to a man when they have sex with them. Most men do not. It is a myth to believe if a woman is good in bed, then she will capture and keep her man. How wrong is this. Sex is the old proverbial "icing on the cake" for a man. What a gentleman really wants is a complete package; sex simply "seals the deal." Some men only want sex and they do not care about the women they are getting it from. Gentlemen are looking for the lady who can fulfill all of the five senses for him: taste, touch, hearing, seeing, and smell (we will explore being a gentleman and the five senses at a later time). A MARE knows if a woman's plan is to get to a man's heart through sex, then all she will end up with is a sex partner not a man-friend, a fiancé or a husband. What she will have in the grand scheme of things is only a broken heart. He may not want anything else from her after he gets what he wants. Again this is my humble opinion, but I know it has happened to many of my girlfriends, their friends and many others.

CHAPTER FIVE

Attractive

S ome of the most attractive women in the world have happiness written all over them. Even when they are facing challenges, they are skilled at not letting it show in a negative manner. I asked a neighbor of mine who is seventy-five years young, how she is doing. You know, a general question. I know she is faced with some of the most challenging situations she has ever had. Her historic home needs many repairs, she is jobless because no one wants to employ her because of her age even though she is the wisest and most able person to work almost anywhere, and for most positions, she is over-qualified. When I look at her, her appearance does not show signs of what she is going through. In her past, she was a radio host and had a nickname, which described her beauty. Today, she is one of the most attractive ladies I know. Not just on the outside, but her persona is attractive. She is not without flaws, however, she graciously embraces her age and is quick to tell others how young she is. Of course she doesn't look seventy-five, but what does being seventy-five supposed to look like?

I am learning women over forty are capable of being sizzling, hot. Women in America are beginning to realize what Europeans men have always recognized; the stable and experienced woman is incredibly sexy. Physical and medical changes are a part of everyone's life, no matter the age. When it happens to the forty plus woman, do not let it keep you from being the alluring, gorgeous person you are intended to be.

My friends who have traveled abroad often make remarks about how European men give positive, encouraging looks and make flattering comments to forty plus women. They say we are sexy, strong and attractive. Attractiveness, however, is more than just looking good. Europeans are aware of the "time tested" woman for her knowledge and her merited outlook. She has challenges, yet does not let them negatively impact her. She has her own personal beliefs and does not depend on others' approval of her. Life has granted her the ability to be confident in herself. She is a lady who takes care of herself, physically and emotionally. It is our stability, confidence, and self-esteem, which come from just living life that stretches us, making us who we are. We are mature ladies not immature women. Europeans men love this. I look forward to my planned trip to Europe. For sure!

The men regardless of their age, who are attracted to a forty plus lady, are not infatuated just because of her good looks; but also because of the upbeat way she conducts herself. The poise and warmth she exudes upon meeting people, and her great energy, attract. These qualities are intriguing to men. She knows herself and is satisfied with who she has become, and what she has accomplished. These ladies possess a plethora of awareness and know-how due to life's valuable lessons.

Ladies forty plus are gorgeous, desirable, established and treasured. Every woman should strive to attain these characteristics thereby becoming a lady.

Men Do Have Emotion – Believe It or Not

Contrary to popular belief, to me anyway, men do have emotions, but put up a wall of pride to block anyone from seeing them. The way to penetrate his wall of pride is through his heart. When ladies make a man "loose his mind," it is a true statement. He lets down his guard and macho ways, and begins to gain feelings, which come from his heart. We do this by being ourselves and not being superficial. We allow a man to see we feel great and take care of ourselves, have a healthy view of the world, and we have emotions but know how to control them, most of the time. Even though we are independent and confident, we know when to allow the man to take the lead and he loves it. This, I believe, is what attracts a gentleman to a lady.

What I also see is when a man is made, comfortable, confident, and not controlled, he feels relaxed. When he is in a relaxed, calm, stress-free, limited pressure situation, he WILL be apt to show his emotions.

I always construct an atmosphere of comfort around anyone and in any situation whether or not I am at work, at home, out with friends, but ESPECIALLY with man. Knowing his world is full of pressure, I create the vibe of coziness. He feels pressure on the job, pressure to provide, pressure to perform, and simply pressure that comes with being a man. Ultimately, he does not want to feel pressure with a woman, and most importantly in his relationship. A MARE causes a man to be at ease when he is with her, thereby offering an invitation to him to feel open. The best compliment she can receive from a man at this point is, "I am very comfortable when I am with you. I feel I can be myself around you." To my credit, I have heard this before. This is why I can share these words with you. Upon receipt of them, I purely reply, "Thank you, and I'm glad you feel this way" See, I told you. A man does have feelings.

A MARE sees these attributes to be true as she keeps an open mind and continues acquiring knowledge and ways to gain a man's heart. When we feel incredible about our beliefs, and ourselves men pick up the vibe and long to be around it.

In doing some research about what really attracts a gentleman to a lady, I encountered a mythical creature called a Siren. There are articles on who or what these lovely creatures had making them so desirable.

"In Greek mythology, the Sirens were sea nymphs who lived on an island surrounded by cliffs and rocks. Their enchanting singing drew approaching sailors to them, causing them to sail off the cliffs and drown. Odysseus escaped the Sirens by having all his sailors plug their ears with wax and tie him to the mast. He was curious as to what the Sirens sounded like. When he heard their beautiful music, he ordered the sailors to untie him but they ignored him. When they had passed out of earshot, Odysseus stopped thrashing about and calmed down, and was released. In early art, the Sirens were represented as birds with the heads of women. Later, they were represented as female figures with the legs of birds, with or without wings. Birds were chosen because of their characteristic beautiful voice. However, later in history Sirens were sometimes also depicted as beautiful women (whose bodies, not only their voices, are seductive), or even as mermaids (half woman, half fish). The fact that in some languages (such as

French) the word for mermaid is
Siren adds to this confusion."[iii]

Women in general, have the ability to be
Sirens. We can attract a man by our beautiful
music. Music being sounds which create a
pleasant or arousing outcome for the hearer,
my definition. Sounds such as even, tempered
conversation, discussing instead of arguing,
commenting instead of questioning and
complimenting instead of tearing down. What
will this do? It will make a man want to be
with you. I find it takes a special woman to
attract and keep a special man. Men like to
think they are in control of their emotions.
They sometimes do not want to admit they are
enamored with a woman. They display a strong
exterior and don't want to lose themselves over
a woman. But if a woman is a Siren, he will
pursue her and risk his tough guy exterior,
freely releasing his desire to remain single
because of his enchantment with the Siren.
A man will go to great lengths to be with
an attractive, independent woman and once he
stumbles upon her, he will never want to lose
her. M.A.R.E.S. are today's Sirens. Just like
the Sirens of old, it does not take special
abilities to be a Siren, just a willingness to
be beautiful on the inside and outside.

Playing Himself to Tears

"Pogorelich was born 1958 in Belgrade. He
studied piano first in his own country and
then in Moscow from age 12, where at 17 he met

his master teacher, Georgian pianist Aliza Kezeradze.

Today he can look back at a 30-year career, which began sensationally in 1980 at the International Frederic Chopin Piano Competition in Warsaw.

The pianist Martha Argerich, who was a member of the jury, protested his elimination in the finals and declared him to be a genius. That same year he married Kezeradze, 21 years his senior and the mother of a child, after she left her husband for him.

Pogorovich went through the 1980s and the 1990s with the aura of an amazing virtuoso who hypnotized audiences everywhere. He recorded discs of works by many composers for Deutsche Grammophon. In 1994, with the help of donors he founded a piano competition in his name in Pasadena, California. The competition was held only once and the two winners received $75,000 each. In 1996 Kezeradze died and Pogorelich withdrew from public artistic activity for a number of years.

In an interview with Die Welt in 2006, he spoke about Kezeradze's importance in his life: "I had to reinvent myself. She was so demanding. She clothed herself in art, she absorbed it, devoured it. She was so universal. She had everything, class, education, beauty, talent and affection. She outshone everything like a comet. You could never stand still with her, that's true, she was always on the go. Even in death she was still the princess she was born as. She had cancer of the liver."[iv]

What a beautiful story. I had to share his words about her with you. I could not re-create how he felt about her. He respected her for who she was, and intensely loved and was in love with her.

This is the way a man falls for a MARE.

---------- ⚙ ----------

What I have noticed is men in their thirties begin to want a serious and committed relationship. Their eyes start to open as they see their male friends around them one by one get married. In their twenties, most but not all men, are still on what I call, "a seek and destroy mission." They are seeking a female who has outer beauty, sex appeal, and some sort of common sense, maybe not. She should like to have fun, party, be somewhat responsible, and have a job. The men are not necessarily seeking a long-term relationship. The ones in this category feel as if they have time when they get older, to get serious. They destroy any thought of marriage because it is not where they want to be. Let's just, "eat, drink and be merry" and later on they will think about marriage.

My take on these guys is their goal whether or not they realize it, is to protect their hearts. There is a fear of loving someone because it is an uncomfortable feeling and not a manly thing to do. To negate and avoid this feeling, they find a woman, and are with her for a period of time, then begin to experience a strange sensation. When this feeling comes, they go. Some men never stay with a woman long enough to begin to experience love. Love is a complex emotion. It requires work. It is quite an undertaking. Ultimately, love and giving your heart is going to cost something i.e. time, energy, being stretched, tension, and struggle. Real love is eventually stressful and takes work. Love requires the giving away of one's heart, and that is not easy. Once love is tested, it then becomes, sweet, caring, nurturing, thoughtful, protective and kind. This takes some time for some men to feel love.

Some men are like a Cyndi Lauper song I heard the other day, in which I changed the words to "boys just want to have fun." The twenty-something, non-committal man is not always set in a career although they may have a job. They are still experimenting with life and will one day plan to settle down, although not yet.

These days some live at home with their parents, and not yet ready to give up the good, and somewhat irresponsible life they are living. There are many men and women who have chosen to live as they desire and this is their prerogative. Touché!

Unfortunately, most women in their twenties accept this behavior. It's not because they like it, but it is because of what they are used to receiving from a man in his twenties. A MARE does not accept this behavior. She knows she deserves more and knows she does not have to settle for immaturity. Having already experienced bad behavior from a former relationship at some time in her life, she knows neglect, mistreatment, possible abuse (being taken advantage of) or disrespect when she sees it coming. How does she know? Because she trusts her own instincts and she may have experienced poor conduct from a man and will not accept it again.

When I was in my early twenties, I had a college degree, my own car, an apartment and by twenty-three, I was married. I happened to find a mature twenty- something man who was ready to be in love, in a committed relationship and eventually get married. Today is a bit different. Some are waiting a little longer and getting more settled in their careers before they take the big step into the married world.

As I mentioned before, the magic age for a man to realize he wants more in life once he has fulfilled his seek and destroy mission is when he is in his thirties. If they are not in a committed companionship by this age, they will continue on until they find it. At times, they may be in their forties and fifties but in their hearts and minds, they now desperately desire love. Love and companionship has no age restriction.

Two male friends are in this boat. One was adamant. He would never get married and would get angry when marriage was brought up. He had married in his early twenties, but it only lasted for one year. There was a child involved in the decision for marriage to his son's mother. A noble event in order to give his son two parents, but it was not for sustaining reasons. Because of this failure, he swore he would never, ever marry again. He had a couple different jobs, started hanging out, had several girlfriends, partied, traveled...until he hit 30, my magical age. When he turned 31, he began to see his male friends in committed and married relationships. I believe he then began to desire what they had.

Another male friend for a long time desired a "love-lasting" relationship. He was the kind of guy with an incredibly, giving heart. There were times he sacrificed his money, time, and effort in order to give to others. In doing this, however, he did not have the resources to open a bank account, establish credit, have a car to drive or did not even have his own place to live. His job paid him enough to support his son and others, but he could barely support himself. When he hit...yes you guessed it...30, his thought processes changed. He had met someone who changed his life, me. A MARE.

He was attracted to my strength, independence, giving heart and responsibility to myself first, then to others. My philosophy has now been equal to what we hear from Flight Attendants when they make the announcement on an airplane about securing my oxygen mask before assisting others. There was a time in my marriage where I put my ex-husband's needs and wants before my own. One day I realized I needed to put on my own oxygen mask and get air for me before I could continue to assist him. This realization aided in my decision to separate from him which eventually ended in divorce. I was lacking oxygen and gasping for air without even knowing it.

When Marc and I became friends, I didn't want him to go down the road I had been down. I wanted him to get his life in order to please himself and not others. After receiving his credit report and us going over it, he realized he had pretty good credit and could afford to make some valuable changes. He developed a monthly budget, opened up a checking and savings account, bought a car and began a bank account to support his son's future educational and developmental needs. Today, he is proud of how far he has come in a short amount of time and continues to thank me for instigating these positive changes to his life.

Needless to say, he was also attracted to me outwardly. We initially met when he worked together on a project. He told me he had a crush on me because I was beautiful. (Does this story sound familiar from an earlier account?) Seriously, I do not consider myself a beautiful or an attractive person. It has been a challenge for me to see this since the fifth grade. An older boy called me ugly and my older brother hit him with a chair for saying this. For some reason, this has stuck with me all of my life. I get teary-eyed just recalling it.

What causes someone to be attracted to another? Many things. I believe a major magnet is comfort. When I am around anyone, I make myself comfortable first. I then apply the golden rule, "Do to others as you would have them do to you." My goal is to be friendly, inviting, mild-mannered, respectful and accepting, regardless of one's socio-economic standing, culture, race, gender, or religious background. I try my best to treat people equally, no matter their circumstances. I am trustworthy, loyal and not a drama queen. I do not have to be the center of attention because I am comfortable with getting the attention of a select few who find me intriguing and captivating.

In my estimation, men are attracted to such attributes. It makes them feel at ease and not guarded; or it makes them feel like they too can be themselves and not put on a fake or superficial persona. I believe men do not respond positively to demanding, attention-seeking women. A man desires a lady who makes them feel manly and proud. Their nature is to support, protect, be loyal to and want to be uplifted and cherished by the person who wins their heart. Societal expectations are demanding enough on a man thus seeks someone with reasonable expectations. He is attracted to a woman who builds him up, not tears him down.

When I was married, I don't remember ever tearing my ex down. In our disagreements, we never hit below the belt. Being prideful, stubborn, deceitful, mean, came up, but not you are stupid, ignorant, fat, ugly, or the like.

Do not get me wrong. A MARE is not a doormat. She does not allow any man to walk all over her. What makes her different is this: She understands how to express her wants, desires, feelings and needs without being disrespectful. In doing this, her gentleman becomes, a gentle man. He wants to know how she is feeling, thinking etc. because she has expressed her heart not her anger, and therefore he reacts positively not explosively.

I have become familiar with self-awareness. At times, it is about me. During the processing of my divorce, and being single, I have an appreciation for concentrating on my personal development and career aspirations. I tell myself to not be more concerned with a man's needs than I am with my own. In knowing my plans, goals, value, desires etc. will make me more attractive to a man. I tell myself to smile more, slightly flirt (which I had never done) and be confident around men and not to fret over what he may be thinking. I continue to identify how to be comfortable in my own skin. If I become this way, then a man would be comfortable with me and into me.

Irrefutably, any woman can be a Modern Siren. We have to believe in and love ourselves first. Our self-love, self-confidence, self-awareness and self-esteem are a magnet, luring the man of our dreams, and more, to us. After a woman masters being a Modern Siren, her next step is to become a MARE. As Emeril would say, she must "kick it up a notch."

Last October, my mother went into the hospital. Her heart rate had significantly increased. She was not sure of what was going on except her heart did not normally beat fast. She ended up being diagnosed with Tachycardia. Tachycardia is a faster than normal heart rate. The electrical signals in her heart were firing to quick.

The Cardiologist performed a procedure to correct the problem and placed her on a new heart medication. While admitted, she was taken care of by a young, male nurse who often inquired about when I would visit. My mother finally figured out the nurse had a crush on me. The next time I visited, he stayed in her room quite a while and discussed her treatment and made other small talk. I could tell by his demeanor I was the object of his affection. Whenever he found me visiting her, he would make it his business to have to check up on her even though he did not have too.

The day she left was a sad day for him. I could tell he wanted to ask me something, but did not have the nerve; or it was not proper for him to break hospital code. As I hugged him and thanked him for taking excellent care of my mother, he stated, "I hope I see you again." I responded by keeping it positive and replying, "You never know what the cosmos hold." He was so nerve I felt sorry for him. A question was at the tip of his tongue, however being as shy as he was, it did not come out. I knew there was an acute age difference and I would have to turn down any request he had made.

After my mother arrived home, she told me he would constantly ask about me and was hoping during his shift, I would visit her.

This is the Siren type attraction a MARE has. While innocently about our daily activity, a younger man finds us attractive inside and out.

It happened again in January of 2016. Due to a record-breaking rainfall, my basement took in an extraordinary amount of water. I bailed water out of my basement from Christmas Eve until the day after the New Year.

I finally had to call for back up, my homeowner's insurance. They sent a response team out. To no avail, the response team could not stop the water from intruding. It was an act of nature.

One of the guys on the response team, a young 25 year old, was very attentive. Whenever I had a question or needed anything, he responded. One day, he asked me out on a date. I responded by saying I could not do a date because I had to bail water, trying to let him down easy. His quick solution was he could come over for a movie. Being the movie buff I am, and I felt no harm in a friend coming over, I said, "Sure and I would supply the drinks and popcorn if you brought the movie."

Let's just say something mysterious happened. The evening before the movie, I called him to see what soda pop he drank. No response, and from that day forward, no response. I hope I had not lead him astray. I am a friendly person and have acquaintances of many ages and races. Maybe my courteous ways were misinterpreted. Maybe he thought I was a Cougar and was on the prowl. Maybe it wasn't about me at all. Maybe to him it was about his own insecurity. I can assure you my intention was above board. I mean, what could or would I do with a man young enough to be my son, and definitely did not make enough money to assist with bill paying. This is not the way of a MARE, however it is another example of how younger men are smitten with attractive ladies.

This incident made me aware of how and when to turn up, or tune down my charm. It is usually innocent, yet it could have too much or was misinterpreted by the young man.

"INSECURE WOMEN DESIRE ATTENTION.
LADIES GARNER RESPECT."

CHAPTER SIX

Respectable and Respectful

don't know who coined it, but I have often heard people say, "in order to get respect, you must first give it." Or, "you must earn respect." At times I surmise these statements are true however, there are times when others will disrespect you regardless if you have given it, earned it, or not. Racism, prejudice, and all types of discrimination fall into this category. It is hard to give respect to those who disrespect a person for no reason other than differences in skin color, race, sex, origin, class (socio-economic status) or religion.

What is respect? I go to old, faithful, Merriam-Webster's Collegiate dictionary, eleventh addition. According to them, respect can mean: 1) high or special regard; ESTEEM. Considered worthy of high esteem: deference. When I use the word respect, I am generally:

1. Valuing someone or someone else's opinion or point of view and I must add when it is moral and rational.

2. Looking at someone's thoughts or action in an admiring way or:
3. Considering or conceding to others thoughts and actions because they are rational and moral even though they may be different than my thoughts or actions.

Respect is becoming a lost virtue like chivalry. One aspect I love about living in the South is you can do business with a lot of business owners based on your word, their word, and a handshake. I do business with contractors and other business owners simply on mutual trust and respect. I once had a plumber do about $2,500 worth of work and did not bill me. I had to contact him to tell him I hadn't received a bill and I wanted to get him paid. (I hate owing money) He had done thousands of dollars of work for me before and he knew I would pay. I respected his work and he in turn respected, and knew I would once again get him paid. Mutual respect.

From a M.A.R.E.S. perspective, respect goes even deeper than business affairs. M.A.R.E.S. are ladies who respect themselves, thus are able to give respect to others. When one holds themselves in high regard, not arrogance, then she feels confident, secure, and feels no need to judge. She can have her own opinion and stick to it, yet can also adapt to some new, honest, and exciting ways of thinking or acting.

Thinking about things I did in my twenties and thirties, they are different than the things I do and believe now. For example, then I would have trusted almost anything my doctors would tell me and would not ask questions. Now, my outlook is different

---※---

Silence Is Not Necessarily Golden

I still love to watch and participate in athletics. Football, basketball, tennis and martial arts are my favorites. I am presently a 2nd degree black belt in Tae Kwon Do and my next goal is to do weapons training. About nine years ago, I fractured a finger and tore my rotator cuff and had to have surgery. Eventually my deltoid muscle tore way from the bone and had to be repaired as well. A year and a half after my fifth shoulder surgery, (I have had a total of seven. That's another story you can read about in one of my other books) I had a disagreement with my prominent, Orthopedic surgeon about what kind of staples he left in my shoulder after he re-attached my deltoid. When I asked him what material they were made of, he told me "it wasn't important." I vehemently disagreed and told him I could have an allergic reaction to them; better yet it was my body and I had the right to know what he had put in it. His nurse in the background gave me a thumb's up sign as he asked her to research what the staples were made of and to call me with the results. I suppose no one ever challenged him on something to him "was not important," but I did. Knowing what kind of staples I had in my body was important to me.

The visits after the disagreement with him are as smooth as butter. There are no hard feelings. There are feelings of only mutual respect. He respects me because I care about my body and not a pushover, and I respect him because of his notoriety in shoulder surgeries on some of the top collegiate and professional athletes internationally. When we see each other, despite the past incidence, we hug. He says I am one of his favorite patients. Respect, earned or given? I say both.

Respect Yourself

Let's switch gears and look at how respect filters into the life of women when it comes to relationships. There are a limited amount of behaviors, which irritate or annoy me. Something high on my list is when women disrespect another woman. It can be racial, cultural, appearance, socio-economic status or age.

There still exists a group of women who think being a "Cougar" is immoral, unethical and inappropriate for a woman forty plus. The word Cougar to some, implies: predator, sugar mamas, a woman who takes care of her man financially, are sex starved, are robbing the cradle, and are old women trying to be young again. While I must admit for a tiny percentage of women forty plus, this has merit. However, the greater populations of women forty plus are simply looking for love and companionship and happen to find it with a man not her age. What's strange about this phenomenon is it's the men who are doing the pursuing. They want women who love and respect themselves thereby able to love and respect others.

The term Cougar, unfortunately, is not a desired term for some women forty plus. Even for us, the term brings about a negative energy. My desire is not to promote another label, term or word for women. We should not have to walk around with a label other than who we are, women, or in some cases M.A.R.E.S., or ladies. I prefer to be called by my name. Society however, sets the pace and makes the rules so why not start a new and more positive campaign.

The mare is a beautiful and graceful horse. She is also strong and powerful. When I think of ladies who exude these qualities, I want to be like them. There are too many ladies to name who fit this category. They are Hollywood actors, musicians, artists, businesswomen, secretaries, assistants, moms, aunts, grandmothers etc. We have heard of them. We respect them and stand in awe of them. They didn't get this way over night. It took time, energy, tears, heartaches and confidence building. That is why ladies forty plus who are M.A.R.E.S. transcend uniqueness. She laughs at others and laughs at herself. She respects others and respects herself. She knows her boundaries.

"TIME IS ON MY SIDE!"

CHAPTER SEVEN

Easygoing and Even Tempered

Reflecting back on my first time on a mare, one of her attributes was her easygoing spirit. She was calm, relaxed and tolerant when I mounted. She did not flinch even when I gave her a tiny spur to the side, which I disliked, to get her going. As we walked to line up with the others on horseback, she appeared comfortable with me on her. The average weight for a seven-years, young girl is about 50 pounds. The average weight for a mare is around 1,000 pounds. I was only .05 percent of her weight, and she probably didn't even notice I was there.

A human MARE, functions in a very similar way. She is charitable and even-tempered, skilled at the spurring of life. She has been poked, prodded, and jabbed as she has jumped over the hurdles of life. M.A.R.E.S. handle the spurs of life just as my mare handled me spurring her years ago, without flinching.

You're Fired

When my career as a Program Manager ended at a job I loved, I was told it was because the position had been eliminated. It was 4:30PM, and I was asked to join my supervisor in his office for a meeting. Upon arrival, seated next to him was the Director of Human Resources. I thought it very odd she would be at this meeting. A quick flashback entered my brain, as I recalled not more than a month prior, a co-worker had been released from her duties. She said she had no clue it was coming because she had received a good evaluation 30 days prior. Suddenly I felt a rush of adrenaline. Was I about to receive a pink slip too? What seemed like a second later and without warning, I was told my position had been "redefined with a different focus" essentially, eliminated. I was stunned. After the initial shock, I asked why and was given a politically correct response of the changes being made in the department warranted my separation.

I was given about an hour to gather my personal effects, and then was escorted out of the building by security. Me, standing 5 foot, 3 inches tall and at an average weight being escorted out by two security guards? Did I all of a sudden become a dangerous criminal who needed to be watched and escorted out? I will pause here and offer some advice. You can either take it or leave it, your choice. Since this incident, I ask my employers to treat me in the same way they hired me if we ever have to separate from each other. Meaning if you hired me with a smile and with pleasure, then I expect to be treated the same way upon exiting. All thus far, have agreed and it has been documented in my employment file. I however, stipulated if I have demonstrated negative and irrational behavior coupled with poor job performance and with proof, and this warrants my dismissal or removal, then I expect to be treated accordingly, but still with respect. Okay, back to being easygoing and even-tempered.

During this situation, I told myself I must be the mellow, steady and calm person I have grown to be. I must maintain composure and remain in control even thought ever fiber of my being wanted to retaliate. My emotional and irrational side said to release my negative energy by whatever means necessary. In the end, my mature and rational side won. I gathered my things, claimed they were too heavy to lift (smile) so security put them in my car (they had to do something constructive) and got in the car.

Finally realizing what had just happened, a tear rolled down my cheek. That was all I had. I was angry and could not squeeze out another tear. After I gained my composure, I drove away. As I left, I thought about what just happened then immediately remembered I was on the hunt for another position within the same company anyway. I was methodically and carefully planning my departure from this position. I soon came to the conclusion I was a little too slow and methodical, according to God. I had kept one foot in the position while testing the waters elsewhere. The elimination of my position was the shove I needed to get on with my life. I had desired a change in careers and wanted to enter the Entertainment industry. I was not sure what I wanted to do.

After the sting of not having a job anymore started to dissipate, I realized I had started a 2nd Bachelor of Arts degree and I needed to finish it. This degree would be the beginning of my new career as a creative artist. Some encouraged me to become an actor but I told them I felt most comforted and passionate about being behind the camera and creating characters. Naturally, I am quiet natured yet passionate. I can go from 0-100 in about 8 seconds if someone gets on my bad side (my mother recently nicknamed me "Flash" because of it). To discover my true directions, I decided to complete my next degree, and then would decide which direction to go.

When I enrolled full-time, I wondered how I was going to pay for tuition and fees at this private university. I decided to take out a student loan to finish the coursework. I received a letter from the university's financial aid department. It was a statement of account and what I owed. I feared opening it, but took the plunge. To my surprise, my balance was only $400. "FOUR HUNDRED DOLLARS?" I exclaimed as I read the letter. This must be a mistake. It should read $12,400. I called the financial aid office and they confirmed what was on the statement. They said after they applied "my scholarship" to my balance, it left me only owing $400.00. "My scholarship!" I had forgotten all about it. This scholarship was the result of being a spouse of someone who was employed by the university in a specialized capacity. It was part of my ex-husband's benefit package he received when we moved from Los Angeles. Thank God.

As a result of already having a Bachelor's degree, it only took a year to complete my second Bachelor of Arts degree in Communication and Media Studies. This degree would be a necessary stepping-stone for me. Soon after completion of it, we moved to New York City for a year so my ex could complete his Master of Science degree at Columbia University. I loved the time in New York, but it was extremely tough finding a job in my new field. Since employment was a bit challenging, once again I decided to return to school to become even more tooled for what lay ahead in the Entertainment industry. To make a long story short, I began and completed my Master of Arts-Creative Writing degree. I fell in love with Screenwriting and Producing. I had always been a Writer at heart, not knowing how to turn my passion for writing into a career. Eureka! I will become a Screenwriter/Author/Producer, and it is what I do today. At the point of completing this book, I have written five scripts in 2 ½ years, which is a remarkable feat. I have also written 3 ½ fiction and non-fiction manuscripts. I have pitched one script and plan to do the same with the rest. I know one day soon something big will happen for me in screenwriting, but until then, I keep writing, praying and pitching.

Why did I tell all of this? I believe in my heart if my position had not been eliminated,

I would still be stuck doing the same old thing and not in hot pursuit of my dreams and reality, which I deem is one in the same. Had I blown up and said or did something crazy when I was told my position was being eliminated, I would not have a clear conscience or criminal record (smile). I remained even-tempered when the situation could have gotten ugly.

I applied the same principle when I was married. My ex and I did have disagreements, believe it or not. Before I allowed myself to go berserk, get loud, use unkind words or be extremely argumentative, I would become silent and walk away. At times, it was hard to clam up and walk, but it was necessary. My dad was like this. I don't remember hearing my parents arguing when they were married. I don't remember him in an ugly battle with my stepmother either. (I don't know how she did it. My dad is not the easiest person to get along with especially when he thinks he's right about something, and that's always.)

In the years growing up, our son only saw us in a heated argument maybe twice? If you don't believe me, ask him. I am a firm believer of children not being a part of parent's disorder. I am not a psychiatrist, psychologist, M.D. or any other professional or expert with that specific training, however I am a parent.

⸻ ◈ ⸻

Mind Over Matter in Relationships

In the heat of the moment a MARE recognizes she has options. She especially employs them in relationships. Most often, it doesn't matter to a MARE what a man thinks and feels about her. Through situation after situation in her life, which has affected her attitude, she takes responsibility for her behavior. Because she values herself, she will not allow a man's negative demeanor or actions to throw her off balance by retaliating or using bad language.

Let's talk again about the relationship between a MARE and the developing man since this relationship is still under scrutiny by many. Because the developing man is in the process of a metamorphosis, his emotional state may fluctuate. He may be emotionally steady at one moment, then switch gears and non-intentionally become thoughtless, physically and emotionally. He may want to be with you one moment, but then want to do something different the next. Most often to a MARE, this behavior is expected so she correctly handles her feelings. She doesn't undergo the sting of what-happened-to-our-time. On the contrary, she has already come to understand the mentality of not just the developing man, but men in general. It takes time and patience to learn what not to say and how not to react without blowing a gasket as some less mature woman would. If the association she has with her mate is not serious, then she will chalk it up as another learning experience. A MARE keeps in mind at that time, there are other options to be pursued.

   I have come to the realization long distance relationships are not for me. What is long distance for me? If either party has to travel over thirty minutes to get to the other one, then it's long distance. I remember a time when my friend was visiting. Because he lived over an hour away, this was definitely long distance, which made my investment in the association, limited. It was good to see and be with him. We generally had a good time when we were together. Cooking, going to the movies, hanging out at different social scenes and special events, laughing, listening to music etc. were a blast. One time the visit was the proverbial the roller coaster ride. One minute it was comfy-cozy and just the two of us, well four if you count my dogs. The next minute it was "I'm gonna go over to Phil's (not his real name) to play the guitar." Ouch, was my initial reaction, which then became a smirk and a laugh. This smirk and laugh was then followed by an okay, and an opportunity to go to my computer to tell you what just happened. A perfect example of the emotional roller coaster a man can exhibit; up one moment and down the next. A MARE realizes again, she has options.
   A man will not think twice of hesitating or dishonoring you when he senses you value yourself, and you will not put up with his bad behavior. He will select you because a MARE is confident in herself. She is most often

enticing because she is self-assured and not egotistical.

He is fascinated, enchanted, attracted and whole-heartedly won over without a MARE doing a thing. Just being with her while she is constantly doing her own thing, and loving herself, will make a man feel like he has won a great prize.

M.A.R.E.S. hold dear the significance of being a confident, self-aware woman, and not tolerating ANY man taking advantage of her or keep her speculating about what is to happen during their time, unless it is a surprise. She always decides the fate of her actions and maintains a level head through the most challenging situations.

⬥

Odd But True Story

One time, a very dear, handsome, gorgeous, developing male friend of mine, needed a place to stay while he completed a project in town. He asked if I would allow him to stay at my place for free. He had limited funds and would not be able to offer much by way of money. Being the kind-hearted person I am, I said, "Sure."

Now two attractive, fun-loving people living in one place can be an issue. It is said a man and a woman cannot be friends without something going on sexually between them. Possible? Hard, but it can be done.

We had different schedules, came and went at different times, and were barely at home the same time. When we were home at the same time, he was in his space and I was in mine. The times we were at home at the same time, I made it my business to not dress alluring, to not walk around the house scantly clothed, and I respected his space. I didn't go in his room without knocking.

One night, however, he was sore from working out. The fireplace was warm and cozy. He had bought some white wine and we were chatting and relaxing. Because I am excellent at giving massages, I asked if he would like one. "Sure," he said as he lay on the floor with cushions to absorb the hardness, of the wood floor. Where were your minds?

I started to massage him and he enjoyed every moment of it. I started at his shoulders and managed to work my way down his back. As he relaxed, he removed his shirt to reveal his muscular back and chest. How could any hot, blooded, female not notice the beauty, and the tightness of his body? I am not prude. I do have eyes and very good sight. Let's continue with the story.

As he moaned, I asked him if every thing was okay. He replied, emphatically, "Um hmm." Was I turned on? Not. Moments later, I found my hands very close to his well-shaped bum. I took the opportunity to see what he had and slightly and methodically, moved his sweatpants midway down, just passed his hips and ever so slightly to expose the rounded part of his tanned buttocks. Being a lady, and always asking for permission (right), I asked if he wanted me to continue. "Um hmm," he replied.

Easygoing and Even Tempered

With the soft light and glowing warmth of the fireplace, he was totally relaxed, and I must admit, so was I.

I straddled him on the floor where he could not see me, however I saw all of him. This gorgeous, hunk of a tanned and toned man was literally at my fingertips. We had more wine and relaxed even more as I continued to explore every inch of him I could. Feeling each and every protein-rich, muscle on his body was a treat to me. I asked if he had had enough and of course his response was, "No way."

I continued to massage his back, each arm and each leg with the gentleness you take with a new, born baby yet with the fervency of a hungry tiger. I massaged every inch of his manliness, except his MANLINESS, if you know what I mean. He was like putty in my hands.

It was getting late and I had to work the next morning. He told me I had the best hands he had ever felt on his body. It was that night I discovered what sensuality meant. Here were two adults. One alluring man and one dazzling female, yet there was no sex.

I understood the closeness you could have with a man without having sexual intercourse. I don't use the word often, but it was an amazing feeling. A feeling, which left no regrets.

After I finished massaging him, I whispered ever so softly in his ear, "Good night," then I kissed his earlobe ever so tenderly. I know this caused the kind of rise he had never felt before. There is an intimate, sensual evening, by a warm, fireplace, without sex? The true marks of a lady, a MARE. I promise you, he will NEVER forget that evening. He will NEVER experience another evening like it.

Okay, after such an intriguing story, you want to know the age difference? Let's just say he was thirty something, I on the other hand, was not.

"BRAINS AND BEAUTY?"

CHAPTER EIGHT

Single, Professional, Extraordinary Ladies

The Sister's Code

Growing up, I often wanted a sister. It didn't matter if she was the younger sister or the older sister, I just wanted someone to be my best and closest friend; a person I would share my secrets.

I had a sister. We only shared a father, nothing more. I didn't see her much. She had her siblings from her mother's side, and I had my brothers from my mother's side. My two older brothers took very good care of me. They taught me to play most sports; we went to movies together, tore up things together and got in trouble for it, together. However, they did not understand girl stuff. They were not a sister.

I had girl friends in elementary, junior high and high school, but no one ever became a sister. The closest person who became a sister to me was my cousin Veronica. We were close because her dad and my dad were brothers and we all spent a lot of time together. My uncle would include us in activities and trips he would often take my cousins. He especially loved taking us to church. At the time, he had seven kids and when you added the three of us, we would fill up two church pews. This made him more confident as he preached on Sunday mornings.

Veronica and I would talk about almost everything when we were together. We most often discussed the boys we loved, listened to music, danced and talked about school. We shared many things but she was still not my sister because we only saw each other some weekends and during the spring and summer breaks.

I finally went off to college five hours away from home. The first semester went well. My boyfriend and I managed to stay in love, I had a 3.5 GPA and the homesickness had dissipated.

The second semester of my freshman year, I became a member of a sorority and finally I had sisters. We were together for eight weeks, day and night getting to know each other intimately. We saw each other at our best and we saw each other at our worst. We argued and we made up. We wore each other's clothes, did each other's hair, laughed and cried with each other. We became close. There was nothing we would not and did not do for each other. There was no distrust, betrayal, jealousy or worry between us. It was all of us against them. After our pledging and ship or hell week was over, we still remained friends.

What I loved and still do love about my sisters, is none of us ever went after or dated another sister's man. We honored the Sister's code. What is the Sister's Code? It is an unwritten code which purely implies a true lady would never violate this code by going after another lady's man; or would not succumb to the advances of a man in a relationship with another woman. Period.

The most detestable characteristic in women to me, then and even now, is when women actively scheme and goes after another woman's significant other, especially a married man. Before you say it, yes it is my belief it is the husband's fault for his infidelity, but a woman who does not respect herself and another woman and purposefully goes after a committed man, is someone who disgusts me. This may be harsh. It is my personal opinion, choice and feeling. You are entitled to have yours whatever it maybe. I have often heard, "opinions are like butts, most everyone has one!"

In defense of women who have no clue of a man's marital status because he keeps it a secret, I say to really get to know all aspects of him, be inquisitive and look for signs indicating something is not quite right. There are times when some women honestly do not know the man is married. There are also times when a woman fully knows a man is married, yet chooses to still pursue and be involved with him. To them I say, be careful because one day the shoe will be on the other foot, and he or another "he" will betray them.

Okay, I hear another question, "What about couples who are just dating? What if a woman pursues or chooses to be with a guy who has a girlfriend?" Hum. The jury for me is still out. There are many factors, which must be discussed before I can give you my opinion. First of all, how is dating described? Casual or exclusive? When it is said someone is in an exclusive relationship, what does this mean to him or her? Describe it in detail to avoid misunderstandings. If you are in a relationship, does your social networking pages say "single" (because you are technically not married) or does your social networking pages say, "in a relationship" because you have intentions of being with this person, possibly taking the relationship to a higher level like marriage status? You have found the one who gets and completes you, and you know you feel like you cannot live with out them. That's just my take. Since I have been both married and single for a significant amount of time (double digits for each), I may have a different perspective on what 'single' means to me, and what 'in a relationship' means to me.

I compare both of these terms to the shoe buying process. The intended length of being with someone, I compare to purchasing a pair of shoes. I believe some people change boyfriends and girlfriends like they go out to purchase a pair of shoes. They are not sure about the shoes until they put them on, walk around and like the price. If, and I mean if, they buy the shoes when they get the shoes home, they may still change their minds and return the shoes. Some approach a relationship in the same manner. They want to see how the boyfriend or girlfriend feels and looks before they get them and take them home. I implore couples to discuss the parameters of their specific association. One may think the shoes are kind of loose so there is some wiggle room, just like our relationship. The other may think the relationship "fits tight like a glove." This is the only pair of shoes for them, and they will never part. Exclusive!

I also plead with both parties in a relationship to know your intentions. If you want to find a mate in order to get married, make it known to your partner. If you have no intention to ever get married, then find a mate with your same intentions. Please don't think you can change your mate's mind about marrying you, only they can change their own mind. And please don't lead your mate astray if you never plan on marrying not just them, or anyone. Allow them to find someone who wants to fall in love with them and marry them. I have seen this happen too many times with too much hurt and too much time wasted for one or the other person. I implore you, please be honest with yourself and be honest with your mate.

-------- ❁ --------

Victoria's Story

"Victoria" met "Mike" at her job. Although there was no interest in him, her continued professional contact soon cast him in a different light. When she was going through a difficult time with her spouse, she remembered an article he had written about his own difficult separation and divorce. She set up coffee with Mike in a public spot just to gain some insight, from a man's perspective, about how men think. To her surprise, Mike was very open with his circumstances causing Victoria to look at him in another way. She noticed how he spoke with compassion, which she thought was out of character for most guys. He shared how he met his ex-wife, when she became pregnant with their son and the sorted details of the demise of their marriage. As Victoria listened to him, she became attracted to him not just because he was incredibly handsome and very easy on the eyes, but he had done something no other man who she barely knew did; He opened up to her. He made her laugh, was compassionate, and gave her suggestions based on his personal experience. She became extremely comfortable in sharing what was going on in her life and listening to Mike, neither noticed the time. When Victoria spilled some of her coffee, Mike quickly got up and raced to her rescue by retrieving napkins for her and began dabbing the coffee off of her clothes. What a gentleman!

At the end of their meeting, there was some special energy happening between the two of them and she felt it. Leaving their meeting place, he motioned for her to go first by slightly bowing, and then held the door for her. Outside as they both hesitated to leave, there seemed to be a desire to stay in each other's company just a little longer, but they both had places to go. Mike motioned as if wanting to make physical contact with Victoria, a simple hug. For some reason, Victoria could not reciprocate and quickly turned to leave. How could this happen in an hour and a half and over a cup of Joe?

When Victoria got home, she sent a text message to him explaining the reason she could not hug him. She admitted being attracted to him and not able to touch him because of her guilty feeling in still being married. She also told him the hesitation was not because of their different race or ethnicity. He responded back and wanted to know why she was just telling him her feelings. She responded about the timing and remaining professional on the job.

From time to time, they spoke over the phone and sent text messages back and forth. The times in which they communicated were wholesome and friendly conversations, nothing risqué or inappropriate. One day as they were talking, Mike told Victoria he had a girlfriend and she at the time was 42 years young. As he chuckled, he told Victoria his girlfriend "was a cougar." "Oh, no." she thought. "This cannot be happening again. Another cougar comment?" Victoria hesitated for a moment and responded by saying she was not a cougar and, hated the term. She explained to him the word had a negative connotation and he apologized. Continuing their friendship even after they no longer saw each other at work, appeared to be their desire. They would see each other occasionally while working on special projects elsewhere, but still Victoria remained in control of her feelings for Mike as they were developing. One day Mike told Victoria he had sometimes a hard time with their friendship because she "made it difficult" for him. Out of respect for herself and her husband, Mike and his girlfriend, Victoria did not question his comment, but strongly felt it was an inference to his mutual attraction to her.

A year into the friendship, Victoria told Mike she had decided to separate from her husband. She had hired an attorney and was filing for a legal separation. This decision was because the emotional strain of the marriage was affecting her physically. It appeared Mike became protective of Victoria evidenced by some of his comments about "Adam," Victoria's husband when she and Mike worked together. Adam had met Mike while on a special assignment for Victoria. When he and Mike talked about a business matter, Mike immediately became upset with a monetary issue. He accused Adam of not valuing his professionalism and refused to deal any further with him. Victoria believed the disagreement was not really monetarily stimulated, but could somehow be attributed to the fact Victoria and Adam were separating. Mike may have felt partial to Victoria, and how harmfully Adam may have been treating her, resulting in the separation. Adam on the other hand, had later accused Victoria of either being in love with Mike or maybe having an affair with Mike. This accusation caused a heated discussion. Victoria adamantly told Adam the separation had nothing to do with Mike. Their marriage had started to deteriorate long before she knew Mike. She told Adam to leave Mike out of any discussion they had, and Adam must take responsibility for his bad decisions. These decisions had finally caused her to ask for the separation. She needed the time to figure things out on her own and asked her husband to move out temporarily.

Initially, he refused to move out of the home, but moved to a nearby place they jointly owned. When Victoria felt this move was not far enough away from her, she asked him to move further away. Again he refused and told Victoria he would only move if she divorced him. Victoria felt backed into a corner and knew the only way she was going to get Adam to leave was to actually file for the divorce.

When the weekend was over, Victoria immediately called her attorney and told her she was ready to file. The attorney asked Victoria if she was sure and she responded it was the only way Adam would leave. Victoria spoke face to face with Adam and told him she felt backed into a corner. He had left her no other alternative but to file for the divorce by his latest comment. He was argumentative, upset and hurt by the news, and stormed out of the room.

When Mike returned from an extended break out of state, he immediately called Victoria, and asked how she was doing in addition to asking her if her husband was gone. He also wanted to know if her divorce had been finalized. She was so surprised by the call she hesitated in her response. A feeling of warmth and excitement rushed through her body. She knew he had just arrived in back in town. It was he. The younger, gorgeous guy she had hidden her feeling from was on the phone with her? She smiled as she realized she was one of the first persons he chose to contact upon his arrival. Removing the phone from her ear in disbelief, pausing for breath, she told him the divorce documents were being completed and they were to be filed within a week. She also told him her husband still lived close, yet would be moving out in thirty days as stated in the separation documents which had been executed a month before. Mike was happy for Victoria, encouraging her to move on with her new life. He would be there for her if she needed him were comforting words he spoke to her.

She diverted the conversation away from her by asking about his time away. It had been productive as he had received some specialized training for his career and had a great time with family and friends. After the conversation ended, Victoria felt a rush of exhilaration resulting from the call from Mike.

Over the next few months at work, Victoria and Mike continued to be in touch. They would see each other in passing and an occasional quick visit from Mike. By this time, Victoria was officially divorced, ready to start her new, single life. Victoria had not been single in a while. She always had a man in her life. Now she had to re-tool herself and learn how to be single again. Mike encouraged her to take it one day at a time. It was peculiar. Whenever Victoria needed some encouragement to move forward, Mike somehow knew and would send a text message of support. He was still in the relationship with his girlfriend and Victoria continued to respect it even though her hidden feelings for Mike continued. Oddly enough, she had a feeling Mike might have possessed some type of emotional feeling for her as well. They were like soul mates, but knew their boundaries. They continued to share personal challenges with each other and knew the other would keep the information in strict confidence. This is what made their relationship unique. Mike knew things about Victoria no one else knew and Victoria knew things about Mike no one else knew. They completely trusted each other and did not betray the trust they shared.

On several occasions, Victoria and Mike worked together in very private settings. The awesome aspect of their relationship was they were never sexually involved. Though she felt there was temptation to be with one another, on her part, both respected their friendship and Victoria respected Mike and his girlfriend.

Victoria's contention had always been she refused to go after another woman's man. However, it was hard with Mike. She had gotten to know him so well. She admired his closeness and love for his family. He was hardworking and went beyond her expectation when he worked with her. He had a passion for his career and it showed in his efforts and determination. He was honest, loyal and trustworthy. She loved his smile, his dancing and deep focusing eyes, and he was captivating.

She didn't expect to see these mature qualities in a man his age, but they were there. She also didn't want to and did not expect to experience such feelings for a man so soon after her divorce. She felt guilty and decided to consciously hide her emotions.

Victoria finally shared her thoughts with a close, sister/friend Maxine. Max convinced her to not bottle up the feelings with guilt and remorse, but to embrace them and learn to manage them. She helped Victoria to realize Victoria's feelings were not intentional, and people cannot tell their hearts who to fall in love with. "Love? Who said anything about love?" Victoria retorted to her friend Max. Max knew by Victoria's actions and words she had a strong attraction to Mike, even if Victoria didn't want to admit it. Even though her feelings for Mike ran deeper than she wanted to admit, she believed in karma - what goes around will come around. This also kept her from sabotaging another's relationship.

On one occasion, Victoria and Mike had some extra time after planning an assignment they were working on. They went to the store and purchased some food for an outdoor grill out at Victoria's. Mike watched over the grill as Victoria prepared the other food. While the meat was grilling, Mike prepared an incredible, mixed drink for them as they waited. As they sat outside, with drinks in hand, they talked about whatever topic came up between them like two buddies. When the food was ready to eat, Mike graciously assembled a plate of food, first for Victoria then for himself. Victoria was surprised when he presented it to her with his signature smile and his hypnotizing eyes, which she loved.

When the meal was over, Mike immediately began to clean up (what a guy!) He started to wrap up the extra food and put it away in the refrigerator, stacked the dishes, (what few there were) in the sink, and began wiping the countertops. Really? He exhibited the signs of a true and grateful gentleman. A definite "keeper." Victoria could not believe her eyes. She responded by leaving the room so he couldn't see or hear her and said, "Please God...he is incredible!" She said this meant she was asking God to take away the feeling for him. After she jumped for joy, she straightened her clothes, gained composure and returned to the kitchen to finish assisting in the clean up. Finishing the cleaning, they went to a different room and sat and relaxed in a big comfy chair, together. Victoria snuggled next to Mike and began to rub his chest in a comforting way, not sexual, but almost like she rubbed her dogs chest. As they both relaxed even more, Victoria began to play with Mike's ear and he smiled. As things got a little more intimate, Mike jumped up and announced he had to leave. Victoria quickly and without hesitation, agreed. She too jumped up and almost beat Mike to the kitchen door, which led outside. Whew! She knew if things went any further, she would be disappointed with herself.

They met again because Mike was handling another project for her. On the last day of the project, they celebrated a job well done with a couple beers, which was special because Victoria did not drink beer. She did it for Mike. After their toast, Mike told Victoria she was his best friend where they lived. To Victoria, those words were special because she knew Mike was a very private person, and had very few people he considered best friends. His besties were mostly his family members.

Days after the almost incident, Mike told Victoria he had taken another job out of state. When Mike was departing for the job, he and Victoria met to say goodbye. Before Mike got in his truck, he hugged Victoria one final time but did something Victoria did not expect. She was wearing very tasteful, but lighter clothing because it was a hot summer night. She had on a spaghetti-strapped top, which bared her naked shoulders. After Mike hugged her, he tenderly kissed her shoulder, smiled and got into his truck. He never looked back. (Sly devil!) Victoria on the other hand was surprised. She stood there for a few seconds, taking in what had just happened. Coming back to earth, she mustered up enough strength to wave good-bye. All she could think about was the kiss, and how special it was, in a tasteful of way.

Today, Victoria continues her friendship with Mike. She says she is sometimes complimentary with him, but not distastefully. She enjoyed making him blush and she believes men need to know how attractive and desirable they are. Like women, they can be self-conscious and less confident until we as women build them up. It makes them feel great about themselves. Mike told her how "sweet" and nice she always was to him. He showed his thankfulness by always making himself available to work with her when she needed him. He went beyond the call of duty and his work for her was always impeccable.

Single, Professional, Extraordinary Ladies

She began to read a book she fell in love with which walked her through how to be in control of her own life, feelings and desires. She wanted more if she was going to be special friends with any man. She wanted a 100% available, gentleman. She wanted a stallion, a champion.

Mike holds an extraordinary place in her heart, and she knows she will never be in a committed relationship with him. She is now open to date other men. She realized maybe Mike was there for support and a great distraction for all she had going on in her life at the time. Her friends constantly want her to meet other guys, but she is uneasy about blind dates and feels when she is ready, the right man will come. She is however, learning to make the most of her encounters with men she meets in a positive way. She is not actively seeking another relationship and I am told she is becoming self-aware, taking the time to discover the part of her, which has been covered up. In her spare time, she is gaining knowledge about the male species and reacquainting herself with the dating world, step by step.

I respect and admire Victoria. She knows her boundaries when it comes to the opposite sex, especially those in exclusive relationships. She has become secure and seasoned in life. Her life experiences have made her a stable and confident lady who can stand firm through the tests of time. She knows one day her true knight in shining armor will come. She knows his armor is being polished, and he is being made ready specifically to meet her select desires. She is patient and established enough and, her lamp has an adequate amount of oil to stay lit until he, her knight, arrives on his beautiful, shiny, black stallion.

Victoria possesses extraordinary character. She is faithful to herself. She says if she's interested in a man and finds he is in a relationship with someone else, she backs off. She is confident enough she will find some one just for her. She chooses not to ever share a man with another woman.

Let me say it again, M.A.R.E.S. DO NOT go after another woman's man. This is a very special quality in M.A.R.E.S. This lady finds the strength to refrain from going after another woman's significant other. This is not to say she isn't strongly attracted to or does not have chemistry with the male, but she respects herself first, the other woman and the man especially if he's a friend.

Oh, I left you hanging. How much younger than Victoria was Mike? 15 years.

Being Professional and Feminine Can Co-Exist

Some may ask, "Well, what's wrong with having a great job, money and independence?" My response would be, "Nothing." It is very empowering to women. The issue becomes when we strive so fervently to get ahead thus becoming excellent at taking great care of everything in our lives, men do not see a need to have them in our lives. To some men who desire to be the providers, they don't feel like there is a space or place for them. Ladies, I admit, I am guilty of this.

With only one income entering the household after I was divorced when there used to be two, I noticed I became survival-focused. The mortgage, utilities, car loan and insurance and many other expenses had to get paid. Who now had the responsibility to pay them? Me. My energy went from somewhat relaxed to ridiculously stressed. It was only recently I noticed how emotionally taxied I was, and my masculine Y chromosome had become the dominant one, now taking over my two X's, determining femininity. I worked two jobs just to make ends meet. Then all of sudden, one fateful day, I was laid off of my full-time job and the rest is history.

On Facebook one day, I took a quiz out of curiosity. It was about determining if I had more masculine ways or feminine ways. I was not surprised when the results of the quiz told me I was more masculine than feminine. This was eye opening. If I was to ever start dating again with the hopes of getting married, maybe, I had to relinquish my masculine ways, and become a lady yet maintain my professionalism. Why? Because I was sending out energy to men I did not need them, and I may not trust them.

An Alpha male, as I like to call him, wants a woman who he feels will take the less dominate role. He desires a woman he can love, protect, provide for and give her security. If we as independent ladies offer the vibe of having it all together by ourselves, then that energy makes a man feel there is nothing he can do for us. He senses no openness and no reliance on and towards him. Ouch! This reliance allows him to be manly and take care of our needs. It makes him feel like we need him romantically and for security.

My Online Dating Story

I finally met a man of some interest, online. My profile stated emphatically I was interested only in a long-term relationship. The week I signed up, I met him. Communicating almost daily, we discussed some topics near and dear to our hearts. A long, distance relationship is challenging for me, yet I figured this might have been different. Meeting him in person, I immediately dropped my guard. I feared being "Cat Fished" meaning he could have been someone and something different than what he purported to be. We had a great time, and wanted to mutually continue the friendship. The second time meeting up, things changed. I started feeling there were others. He took calls when I was with him, which sounded to be more than business. These calls aroused my suspicion, then my female intuition heightened. I began building walls of distrust. Conversations shortened, more texting started, and I knew this was the beginning of the end. He was my alpha male. He was my protector, my security guard and my manly man, which I needed. I mean, he opened doors for me, walked with me on the sidewalk holding my hand, but placed himself between the street and me. He made my cup of coffee just right and, brought it to me. He gave me a sweet kiss on my forehead in the morning if we were together, and always either text or called me to say, "Good night, pleasant dreams," when we were a part. What happened?

Well, I take responsibility for my part. My alpha, female and Y-chromosome took over. My intuition came to the forefront and gave me signs, which were correct, but the way I handled the situation was not correct. A piece of advice: Never communicate a serious topic by text! This is the way most guys/males and some females, handle things. Wrong. By no means does this mean you allow a man to take advantage of you. It meant I should have let him explain to me what was going on, and for me to not jump to my own conclusions. I should have had a verbal, conversation before ending the friendship via a text message, which coincided with the masculine gene. This encounter had nothing to do with my career. It screams strong, independent, you-are-not-going-to-hurt-me-first man, syndrome, coming from a female.

I understand now femininity is not who I am, but how I am perceived; how I act. Femininity is an act of allowing a man to feel needed, but most importantly, he needs to feel wanted. Real men want a woman who radiates, is soft, genteel, willing to trust him, open, vulnerable, unselfish, sensitive, and real, first. He then can be supportive of our career, strength, self-awareness, and position. He wants us to be an addition to who he is, make him a better person as he makes us the envy of all of those who are in our circle.

Nevertheless, professional ladies, it is not our careers getting in the way of having a meaningful, loving, and marvelous relationship, it's us. It's not about who we are; it is about how we act. I have changed my mind-set about femininity, and ask you to join me in this endeavor. Professionalism and femininity can co-exist, IF we decide to take the steps to make it happen. Tina B. Tessina, Ph.D., a licensed Family Therapist in Long Beach, CA. and author of *The Unofficial Guide to Dating Again,* told WebMD: "For the most part, the men like the sophistication and life success of their older mates." Tessina says, "Other reasons underlying this expansion of dating choices include:

- Older women are looking better every day, thanks to creative, medical, advances and a gym on every corner.
- Women are more likely to come back on the dating market because of divorce and a longer expected lifespan.
- Not as many women are looking for the picket fence and two cars. Now companionship, travel and fun are desired."[5]

CHAPTER NINE

Men and Statistics Speak Out

Ah, how refreshing it is to have the Internet provide access to research while sitting at home on a rainy day, sipping coffee, and being a comfort to your dogs during a thunderstorm.

But as promised, I wanted afford some facts to you about developing men and mature women relationships.

Jean Lawrence, a medical journalist based in Chandler, AZ., published an article on WebMD. Lawrence states through research, "Braving "robbing the cradle" jokes, almost one-third of women between ages 40 and 69 are dating younger men (defined as 10 or more years younger). Lawrence also reports, "According to an AARP poll, American Association of Retired Persons, one-sixth of women in their 50s, in fact prefer men in their 40s."

Psychology of Women Quarterly Journal in 2008 finds: "Women who are 10 or more years older than their partner report more satisfaction and relationship commitment compared to women who are the same age or younger than their partner. The success of these age-gap romantic relationships may be attributed to the vitality the younger man brings into their lives and the maturity and confidence men find in their older counterparts. Moreover, regardless of the age, men seem to be more strongly drawn to these relationships at the start because of physical attraction." Lizette Borelli, author of an article she wrote on January 15, 2015 entitled: "Age Is Just A Number to Younger Men Who Now Prefer Dating Older Women" presents the data by the journal.

In another article, "Older Women, Younger Men" Beth Witrogen McLeod gives us this: "Thanks to higher divorce rates and higher percentages of people who have never married, today 40-percent of the 97 million Americans 45 or older are single. Research on dating habits of these 40-plus singles is sparse, but according to an AARP survey of 3,500 older singles, 34 percent of women in the 40-69 age group date younger men." Something Lawrence also reports.

Let's Hear It From The Boys

Felicia Brings and Susan Winter write a book titled, "Older Women, Younger Men: New Options for Love and Romance." Purchasing the book a couple years ago, I am so glad they have done the research for me and for many others who wonder what younger, developing men think about a relationship with mature women. It is a comprehensive book. It shares statistics, results of interviews with men and women, and offers advice to men/women who indulge in age gap relationships. If you are thinking of such a relationship, then may I suggest you purchase this book. It is a great read, and visit Susan on her site at: www.susanwinter.net

In 1995, the Los Angeles Times reports 23.5% of American women were married to younger men, and with women ages 35-44, this number is close to doubling. This statistic is true BUT... this is 22 years ago. Surely women today in this age bracket in relationship with developing men, has doubled.

What do the guys think? What do they say in reference to being a relationship with these women. Well, wonder no further. Brings and Winter records some quotes directly from younger guys. They tell us exactly why they adore mature women.

> "Friends and colleagues all admired my decision to have a relationship with a mature woman. They respected what I had with her, which was an emotional connection with an experienced, centered person. Most people's reactions have been good. There have been no negative attitudes or comments given to me that stick out in my head. Actually, many people have asked my partner and me for advice" - Patrick, 34.

> "Negative's what negatives I cried I laughed I went back for more.

The advantages can be summed up into two words intense marathon." - Zack, 32

"Advantages of having sex with an older woman? Are you kidding? An older woman is more sure of herself and brings that to the relationship she knows what she wants and how to communicate that to her partner. I like not having to worry about pregnancy or unwanted child. I do not feel the desire to have one and the lack of anxiety over that issue is relieving. Lisa is also in her prime and we have the most intense sexual relations I have ever had." - Gary, 39

"I learned how to make love to a woman. She took me by the hand and said, 'Slow down.' I mean, I was 20- and at 20 you're just so happy to actually be doing it? You never think about how." - Rick, 27

"Fred gave us a wealth of information over several interviews. Open, upbeat and extremely handsome, he revealed the enormous love and respect he shared with his former partner, and now shares with his current partner.

Fred's older woman experience occurred when he was 21 years old and Gretchen was 37. They lived together for two years. They are both still very close and see each other regularly.

Men and Statistics Speak Out

Not only did they have a tremendous friendship as the basis of their relationship, but an extraordinary sex life as well. Recently, this woman underwent major surgery, and it is her ex-boyfriend Fred, not the woman's current older boyfriend who was by her side. Gretchen, now 44 was involved with a man of 51 and he was simply too busy with work and personal commitment to be available when she really needed him. It was Fred who visited her on a regular basis and saw to it that she had what she needed during her recuperation.

After his relationship with Gretchen ended, Fred tried dating girls in their twenties. He explained, often quite humorously how ridiculous he felt trying to have a meaningful conversation over blaring music at a dance club. His brief experimentation with the younger females only reaped endless head games, confusion, and immature behavior. Resolutely, Fred abandoned the "young woman trial period." He knew he liked older women and that was his standard. He decided this time to except it.

His next relationship was with Marla a coworker. They were great friends and then she began to pursue him. Why not? He thought. She was older. Maybe it would work. But Marla's flaws seemed to be that she was only five years older- and for Fred, that still wasn't enough to produce the kind of emotional maturity and depth for which he searched. After a year or so of taking a "time out," Fred met Lynne. She is 10 years older. Friends respect and appreciation of older women was clear when he spoke:"

"The way mature women carry themselves show they know who they are. It equates to stability. They have already figured out who they are. Maybe not all the time, but a lot more often then younger women. They are all around much more attractive to me.

Also they are much more experience deal with life. You know this is the kind of person who is going to tell you exactly what they want and they are more sure of themselves than the people my age or younger. Older women are much more well rounded. They know what they feel and why they feel it.

It is easier to have a relationship with an older woman because she knows how to communicate what she wants. It has a snowball effect all the way around.

I have a preference for women starting at about 10 years older than myself and up. It's an adventure for both of us, because it is a whole, new, exciting journey. Younger women just do not allow me to grow in the ways older women do." - Fred's story.

"I got more of a reaction from men than women. The man of my age and older were jealous that I was with her. They won't look at me as if I had something they wanted and did not have and, because I was younger, they reacted more strongly. And women my age disapproved of the relationship.

Every morning, I would wake up happy and feel like I have the world on a string. I guess some of these people thought I was trying to prove something, I wasn't. Our relationship just made me feel great. She was great! I was proud of who she was and what we had together." - Barry, 26

"If I look at a girl in her twenties, I might find her attractive, but my thoughts are only on sex. I cannot really do anything with her. She is not born yet. She is like a lump of cold clay, very pretty clay, but still unshaped. When I look at an older woman, I see a real woman. They feel like women. They are solid. Their bodies are solid. Their thoughts have solidified. A relationship with an older woman can be very rewarding." - Mel, 32

"The biggest advantage is that they know what they want so there is no guesswork. You may try to please them and they will tell you if it is not working. I love it. That is a turn on. Absolutely no negatives about sex? It was the best. The best!" - Scott, 25

"Phenomenal! The sex was important, but I really was concerned about what she needed and desired. She would take over and go from there. It made things a hell of a lot easier, because we were just there to have fun. It was like breaking through a major barrier that takes other people forever to figure out. There was a 'click' sexually. It was easy and it was great!" - Russ, 29

Fred who was mentioned earlier, expressed his own fulfillment: "Although my initial fear was that I would not be good enough sexually, my larger fear was that I would overwhelm her, like call too many times a day or say one too many 'I miss yous.' Instead, our mutual pleasure went from one high to another."

"I find that I am attracted to a woman who has some degree of self possession. I like the stimulation of a sharp intellect. I enjoy sitting down to dinner with someone who has a level of conversation I can appreciate and enjoy. I think younger women are sometimes too focused on starting families and that is really an issue these women. I have always had relationships with older women. They know themselves. They have so much more to offer, and they are looking for some thing different. They are not just looking for guys who will be good fathers and providers. Older women can be more playful. They are more relaxed. It is really a personality thing for me regarding what is attractive. I enjoy a confident attitude and older women definitely have the upper hand in that area." - Nigel 37.

Dan, who is 24 says: "When I meet a woman over 30, she is usually very clear and focused. She knows what she wants in life, and that makes being with her so much easier. I look at a lot of my friends who have girlfriends their age and younger, and the problem that they have strike me as ridiculous. They frequently act foolish and immature. I do not have time for that behavior. That is why I like mature women."

Art, 27, says: "She was very beautiful and caring, and we had similar interests. She offered me the opportunity to see other perspectives on a lot of different issues. I mean, older women think differently on certain issues, and they have got more experience. I grew up a lot with her. Yeah, definitely, she helped me to grow up. She made me realize how important I could be in making someone else happy. Not that I was doing it for her, but just being with her."

"I met Karolina at a party given by some friends. When I saw her, I thought she was just the perfect woman for me, and I was sure about that. I was not looking for an older woman and Karolina was not looking for a younger man, but it just happened. I was 39 and she was 55 then. Our relationship is unique, because it is not just built on sex, but to trust, respect, and love. We are both morning people and nearly always in a good mood. We are both hard-working with many hobbies in common. In my opinion, age has nothing to do with our relationship. In our 25 years together, we have never had serious problems and we are still very happy." - Paolo 64

"Pat is very special. Not only is she beautiful, but she has a wonderful sense of humor and is a very giving. The ability to talk about anything with her was refreshing and engaging. In fact when I first met her, I did not know

I was attracted to an older woman.
I knew she was older than I, but
I did not realize the disparity in
age until she told me which did not
happen until a couple of dates into
our relationship. Pat offered me
space, devotion, and herself which
I could not find and anyone else.
I take better care of myself now.
She is a best friend who reflects
back to me what a good person I am,
which builds my confidence and self-
esteem. I now have a better job and
feel better about myself than ever
before." - Neal 35

Bring and Winter in an article from www.
today.com, November 8, 2011 holds, "The men
to whom we talked about the men they spoke
about the advantages of being in relationships
with older women in terms of serenity and
comfort, the growth opportunity and the
honestly they were afforded. But more than any
other advantage, they talked about the positive
sexual relationships they experienced. They
all commented that sex with older women was
better."

So there you have it. Real men. Real thoughts.
Real conversation. These men truly honor their
women. I am sure all associations did not
turn out positive. Unsuccessful relationships
are not only problematic in mature women and
developing men relationships, but it happens in
relationships of all ages, colors, religions,
and cultures. What I am sure of is more and

more younger men are finding love, commitment, and confidence in dating and/or marrying mature women. There may not be a copious amount of data taking any more, and maybe this is a good thing. Maybe society is finally starting to silence itself on this trend because it looks like it's here stay.

"The biggest challenge after success is shutting up about it." — Criss Jami

CHAPTER TEN

Confessions of M.A.R.E.S.

Now is the time I will share a story or two of my own. Yes, they are true accounts of some of my M.A.R.E.S. moments. I laugh, tear up, and delight in re-telling them. I hope you get a glimpse and understand why I recount these stories to you. I will use alternative names for the gentlemen who are a part of them to protect their privacy, and because one of the names I do not know.

Story # 1 - Chivalry Is Not Dead

After several days of feeling ill, which is a rare occurrence for me, I decide to have a freshly made tossed, vegetable, salad for dinner. It had been a long, full day at school. After reading thirty essays from my students, I'm exhausted. Not being able to finish my salad, I slip the remainder into the refrigerator to save it for another day. It would not get soggy because I usually don't put the dressing directly on the whole thing. The salad dressing tasted peculiar, but I am trying something different. I chalk it up to newness.

I take my boys for a quick walk to the little park down the street, and on our way back, I begin to feel light-headed. Making it back safely, I call my friend "Bob" (Can I get any more generic than that?) to tell him about my day.

> Bob: Are you okay because you don't sound right? You don't sound like yourself.
>
> Me: Pausing for a moment to take the leashes off of my dogs, Yes, I'm okay. I had a long day, and all of a sudden I just have a little tummy ache.
>
> Bob: That's odd. I never hear you talk about being sick.
>
> Me: I'm sure it will pass. Did you get off work early?
>
> Bob: No, the usual time today. Five o'clock.
>
> Me: Good. So you've been home about an hour?
>
> Bob: About that.

I begin to feel nauseous, and at the same time my stomach start bloat.

> Me: Bob, I have to go. I'm feeling nauseous...

Without waiting for his response, I throw my phone on the bed and make a b-line to the bedroom. A few minutes go by, and I go to my phone. Bob is still there.

> Me: Hello?
> Bob: Are you okay?
> Me: No. I seriously don't feel well.
>   It must be some I've eaten. The
>   dogs have been out and I'm done
>   grading papers I'm going to take
>   bath then lie down. Maybe it
>   will pass.
> Bob: Call me back when you are out
>   of the tub but before you go to
>   sleep, okay?
> Me: Will do.

Running the water in the tub, I drag myself into it. I have no strength. Now I know something is wrong. Should I call 911? Or should I just wait it out? I'm tough. I will wait it out. I fall asleep in the tub. When I wake up, I have no clue what time it is, or how long I have been asleep. I put on my PJ's, get in the bed, and then call Bob.

> Me: I am even worse. I fell asleep
>   in the tub and don't know how
>   long I was out. I feel horrible
>   and I don't know what's wrong.
> Bob: Well, it's 7:10 so if you got
>   in the tub right after we spoke,
>   you were asleep 'bout 45 minutes.

> You sound even weaker. Baby,
> what's wrong?
>
> Me: I don't know. It's not my diabetes.
> I checked my glucose. I don't
> want to go to the hospital for
> nothing...
>
> Bob: It's not nothing...forget it.
> I'm on my way...
>
> Me: No. It's an hour and a half drive
> for you, and you just got off
> work not too long ago...
>
> Bob: I said, I'm on my way.
>
> Me: Okay. Okay. I'm drifting off and
> may not hear you so I will unlock
> the back door. I'm not worried
> about any criminals. The boys
> will hear them.

I then doze off.

I don't know what time it is, but I hear someone asking if I am okay. By then I am curled in a fetal position on my bed because the pressure in my stomach is unbearable. I'm feeling and looking like I am 12 months pregnant, yet I know there are no such phenomena.

Bob finally comes into view, and seems very worried. He takes off his shoes and climbs into bed with me, fully clothed. He is aware of my rule which states only my new husband is allowed in my bed. I am at this point unable to hold my head up or speak, but still refused to go to the ER.

Bob gets up after a while, and goes potty. He then returns. He holds me for a little while, and it feels comforting.

Confessions of M.A.R.E.S.

> Bob: I ain't going anywhere. I will
> be right here.

Sometime in the middle of the night, he disappears. I get up to go potty, and I see something on the floor. When I turn on the night-light, I see it's Bob. He has made a pallet of pillows and blankets next to the dogs' bed, and is sound asleep.

Still feeling ill, I stumble into the bathroom. The next thing I see is him standing there making sure I am okay. When I finish, he escorts me back to bed, and asks if I want anything. He goes downstairs to grab something to eat and drink.

Returning, he kneels to lie on the floor again, but I catch him. I point to the guest bedroom, and demand he goes to sleep there and not on the floor. I remember him saying he wants to stay close to me, but I insist I'm better. I tell him he needs to get some sleep because he has to go to work in a few hours. He says okay, however before he leaves he kisses my forehead and says he loves me. I smile at him and drift back to La La land. It is about 1AM.

About 5AM, I hear something and the dogs do too. Bob is calling the dogs to take them for a walk. They get up, and run out of the room. I'm still a little weak, however my tummy is better. Samm and Theo beat Bob back to my room. He comes in and asks me how I'm doing. Better I tell him. He says he has to leave for work yet will stay if I need him to. I say, I'm good and for him not to worry. He is teary-eyed and has a worried look still. I convince him I am okay, and for him to get going so he's not late. He gives me an incredible hug, and a longer kiss on the forehead, then turns to leave. As he exits my bedroom door, he says, "I love you, and I'm in love with you," then he walks out to drive another 1 ½ hour back home, change clothes for work, and to have only slept four hours.

Bob was extraordinary. He, about a month later, asked me to marry him. As selfless, good-looking, charming, hardworking, attentive, and dedicated a man he was, there was 19 year age difference, yet it wasn't his age. It truly wasn't him. I had only been divorced a little over a year. I was not yet ready to entrust my heart and life to anyone at that point. I also had just begun to enjoy my new found freedom as a single lady, and not ready to give that up.

Why was I sick? I had developed a copious amount of food intolerances and some allergies due to not making enough stomach acid to assist in the digestion of food. My food would sit there and compound without the necessary enzymes to breakdown the food eaten. I also had a mild form of gastro-paresis. The muscle, which releases food into the small intestines after it's broken down in the stomach, was not working properly either. I, in essence, had too much food in my gut not getting broken down, and sometimes just sitting there not being released, thus the fullness and the bloating. Thanks for wondering.

Story #2 - Derrick and Loren

Derrick and Loren claimed to be soul mates. They met one day hot, summer day when he went to repair her air conditioning system. He was in his late twenties and had been planning in his mind, how he would meet his bride. He was old school and traditional in thinking and planned almost everything in his life. For a twenty-nine year old, he was doing well for himself. He had steady income, his own apartment, a car, and a nice amount of savings. Wanting to make sure he was financially sound, physically fit, and of good character, he had not dated seriously because to him he had not encountered the "one," until that day.

Loren, who had celebrated her fortieth birthday, had been for a walk around the neighborhood. She wanted to exercise in the morning since it was getting hotter by the minute. When she returned from her walk, she noticed it was usually warm in her home. Immediately going to the thermostat to alter the setting, she noticed it was already at a temperature, which should have been sufficient for the weather condition. Again, she changes the setting to see if the unit would come on.

After showering and getting dressed, she eventually noticed the temperature had not changed, and she had not heard the AC unit kick on. Loren went to the phone to call her usual company, but it would take until the end of the day before they could send someone out.

A few hours later, the doorbell rang. She went to the door, and opened it to find a handsome repairman standing there. She was speechless. He too paused for a brief moment, and then told her he was there to repair the AC. The two were giddy, and felt a bit nervous. Upon completion of the repair job, she paid her invoice and thanked him for coming. He said it was his pleasure, and they both smiled as she walked him to the door.

Days later, Derrick called her. He had gotten her number off of the invoice. He first apologized for taking the liberty of phoning her. He said he knew it was against company and his own rules to call her, but he could not get her out of his mind. She was cordial and forgiving because he did sound embarrassed and sweet. He told her it was as he said, a pleasure to meet her and he really meant it. He asked her if she would have coffee with him, soon. Loren was surprised by the offer, hesitated for a moment, and then said she would meet him.

Loren had been divorced for over two years, and had just decided it was time to start casually dating. The divorce was a joint decision so there was no animosity or ill feeling towards her ex. She wanted time to do the things she wanted to do before another relationship with a man started. The time with Derrick was what she needed. He was handsome, polite, appeared to know his job well, and was engaging. She would give him a shot.

Derrick, on the other hand, knew the minute he saw her there was something different. When he saw her, heard her voice, and saw how simple yet elegant she was and lived, he KNEW she was the one. He had heard his friends and family telling him that, but he didn't believe it. He thought it was going to take work and many dates to find her, but there she was. He knew it was her in the flesh, right before his very eyes.

The first date at the coffee shop went well, according to Derrick. He felt the chemistry right away. Loren had tons of fun. It was the first time she'd been with a man and had a great time in a while. She liked him, but she wouldn't say she had immediate chemistry.

However, after a few dates, she felt something magical. He was easy to talk to, opened doors for her, pulled out her chair at restaurants, picked things up for her when she accidentally dropped them, and was often on-time when meeting her, but called if he was going to be a tad late. Thinking he was too good to be true, she asked him about his relationship with his family. Derrick was very close to his family. His mom and dad were still married after thirty-five years, he had two sisters and a little brother who was twenty-two. His family lived close by, and they saw each other a few times a month. He even had a wallet with family photos. Go figure!

After drilling him, in a positive way, Loren began to feel less anxious and more interested. One day, without asking, he told her he was twenty-nine, but almost thirty. He knew she was a bit "older," but didn't know what her age was. She told him she would be forty-one soon and loved her years. He could tell. She embraced them like a champ. This made him even more captivated by her. Full of life and able to admit her true age magnetized him more.

They exclusively dated for a year. Loren found herself wanting to be with him more, and he felt the same. He knew what he wanted in a women, and she now knew she wanted him. One month after, Derrick told Loren he knew what he wanted, and she was the only one he wanted. He told her he loved her from the very day he came to repair her air conditioning unit. He then asked her to marry him.

The proposal was adorable. Dressed in his work uniform, he rang her doorbell. When she opened the door, the entry way was filled with flowers, candles, and a new toolbox, filled with tools. For every tool he handed her, he shared the purpose for the tool in relation to how he would take care of her. The final tool was the engagement ring. Awww! He explained to her his world, with all the tools, would not be complete without her. Getting down on the traditional one knee, he asked her to marry him, and the rest is history.

Derrick and Loren have been married now for twelve years, and they even now act like newlyweds. It is refreshing to watch them as they recant their story. Derrick is gorgeous, and Loren compliments him. Who would know there is any age gap between them? They credit their deep, loving commitment to each other as the key to the fountain of youth. Loren says they spend a lot of time and a lot of energy on their relationship, and feels it is worth it. Silly, fun and some times adventurous dates, romantic vacations, and at times relaxing at home are important to them. Whenever they have conflict in the marriage, and they do have it Derrick says, they separate and cool off, then come back to discuss it. Or they might enlist some friends to help shed some light. Loren also says the keys to their love for one another, "great intimacy, great romance and mind-blowing sex." That's a direct quote!

Both of them continue individual development, which enhances their love. Loren loves to read at home and take an art class. Derrick loves to help his friend restore classic cars. This is the way they get "me" time to indulge in the things they independently like to do.

When asked about children, Loren has not been able to carry, however they are in the process of adopting. Derrick seems a little disappointed, but he says he loves Loren and sticks by her. What a guy!

Here's a story of another MARE who encounters her prince when she is not seeking one. Permit me to point out she is at home in dire need of her air conditioning being fixed when HE comes to HER door. That's how it happens with a MARE.

Story #3 - It's Just My Imagination?

It had been a challenging, brutal week in September. It seemed like everything that could go wrong, did. You know the saying of something happening, "when hell freezes over?" I felt the icicles forming from earth. Hell was in the process of freezing over. My home wasn't selling, the bills were due, the money to pay them was not there, and I was two months out from my seventh shoulder surgery.

I received a call from my sorority, line sister informing me of two others coming to Atlanta: one to visit her biological sister, and another who was already there doing research for her doctorate degree. The former would arrive in two days, and she wanted me to come up and meet them for dinner. My sorority sister I was speaking to was excited they were visiting, however I didn't immediately share in her enthusiasm. I had been honest about my state of being before with her, so she offered solutions just to get me to travel the two hours to Atlanta.

I knew her well. We were pledges/pledgees at the same of a sorority in college. At that time, ten of us spent approximately twelve weeks together becoming a part of this sorority. When I say we knew each other, we KNEW each other. When she and I moved off campus a year later, we lived next door to each other. Partying, laughing, hanging with our friends, studying, and eating together made us even closer.

After college and earning her master's then doctorate, she became a Professor at a state university. She had become my mentor, my confidant, and my friend since I had recently become an instructor at another state university, and she was teaching me how to survive academia. She began mentoring me in class preparation, lesson planning, grading, what computer software to use, and the like. The most valuable talks over the phone were about student behavior and classroom decorum. We spend hours talking about these two subjects. We also reminisced over the good old days in college, especially sorority life. This was another bond we shared. Okay, now we will fast forward...

The day came when we were to meet for dinner. She phoned me early in the morning to see what I had decided. I thanked her for telling me about the celebration, but I declined the invitation. I did not want to face the Atlanta traffic at the time of day I needed to leave, and if I were coming, I would have to find a sitter for my dogs. She knew I was making excuses and already had a plan for me.

She told me I could take a commuter bus to Atlanta, grab a cab at the bus terminal, take it to the restaurant, and arrive in time for the festivities. When I arrived at the restaurant, she would come out with an envelope of money. The envelope would have money to pay the cab driver, include enough money for dinner, money to cover the trip to Atlanta, the trip back home, and money to pay the pet sitter. My other sister doing research for her doctorate had a hotel room with two queen-sized, beds where I could kick up my heels for the night. Wow!

She did have it all planned out. I was not surprised. This is the kind of person she was. What could I have said? Well, I said to give me an hour to contemplate the plan. I would allow the spirit to lead me.

Exactly one hour later, my phone rang. Yes, it was her calling. Before I could speak, she empathized with what was going on in my life. She told me how she admired my strength and courage in the battle I was facing, and instructed me to hold on to God's unchanging hand because He would deliver me. When? She did not know, but she assured me He was able.

Luckily, my pet sitter was available for the evening and morning. My biggest excuse was no longer an excuse. I dried my eyes, took a deep breath, and prayed. I conceded and thanked her for all she was doing and had done.

The plan went on without a hitch. When I arrived at the restaurant, I was sure my face was puffy from all the tears of the day. I walked in composed not because I had it all together, but God had pulled it all together for me. I was thankful.

Everyone was glad to see me. We hugged and laughed. They were finishing their meal when I walked in and a young, male waiter came over to the table with a menu. I quickly found what I wanted and ordered it. Barbeque ribs, coleslaw, green beans and a side salad, happy food. After taking my order, he smiled and went away. At the table we chatted it up, looked at some photos on phones, listened to music, and snapped our fingers. It was a great time. I was so grateful to have come to Atlanta. My tears went away and my happy face returned.

A few minutes later, my food arrived. The young waiter waited for my response. The ribs were cold, I responded, and he immediately took them back to the kitchen. He brought them back again, however this time they were just right. I gave him the thumbs up to say everything was fine. He went away and came back in what seemed to be a few minutes. He inquired again if the meal was to my satisfaction. Once again I responded positively.

Talking and laughing with my girls, and finally finishing my meal, the young waiter appeared again. This time he was there to take away my used plate and flatware, then asked if I was having some dessert, sweets for the sweet I heard him say. I declined. Moments later he appeared again, this time with nothing in his hand. I assumed he would bring my check because another waitress had brought the others. He leaned down and began to whisper in my ear. He couldn't see my face, yet my sisters could. They looked at me as I looked back at them.

"May I have this dance with you before I get off work?" was what he asked. I know I must have stuttered when I said sure. I laid the cloth napkin, which I had in my lap, on the table and got up to dance with him. We danced to a couple songs and spoke back and forth while moving to the beat. As we talked on the dance floor, I found he was from Atlanta, a musician and waiter. I also found out he was 25 years old, yes, twenty-five. When the music stopped, I thanked him for the dance as he escorted me back to the table. He was able to ask me if I was from Atlanta and I said I was visiting for the night, simply having dinner with my sorority sisters. I could tell he was disappointed with my words. He thanked me as well for the dance, and said if I ever came back to Atlanta come to the restaurant to see him. I nodded and said I would.

Of course when I got back to the table, I was the joke of the evening. They asked me if I knew him. I said no. They asked me if I met him coming in? I said no. They finally stated he had come from nowhere. He was not their waiter, and they had not seen him prior to me showing up. Immediately, the sister who had sponsored me smiled and said, "There you go again. Attracting these young men." I assured her I was innocent. I reminded her she knew the type of week I was having, and I had been in a somber mood most of the day. Tears had flowed, and I was sure my face was rounder than normal due to crying. I had no reason to believe my beauty was what the waiter had seen. Perhaps he saw by my façade, and came to conclusion I required a boost. He probably felt compassion, as my face was morose/sad. Or, perhaps he was a smile sent directly from God to cheer me up.

All in all, it was one more MARE moment. A lady going about her day, when a younger man takes notice, swoops down, and is mesmerized by something she possesses.

"M.A.R.E.S."

FINALE

Wow! That's it? I cannot believe I am done. I guess I'm really not done because the second part of my personal life is just beginning, and this book is only a snippet of what is to come in regards to relationships. I feel the beauty of this undertaking is the personal perspective from which it is written. I could have inserted a lot of research, data, words and accounts from strangers and what happens to them from a third person view point, but I wanted this to be personal so when you meet me, you can ask me questions or share relatable experiences because I've been where you are, or maybe I am still where you are.

M.A.R.E.S., the special class of ladies who exceed the stigma of ladies forty plus being predators, is an extraordinary undertaking. Why? Because we do not care what others have to say. Love and relationships have no age (except when it comes to the law). I am constantly seeing there is a limited pool of men around or close to my age. Most are either married with children, divorced and want to have relationships with many women to soothe their egos, emotionally unavailable or looking for the twenty- something, trophy woman etc., etc., etc. I know somewhere there are stable, lovable, financially, sound, men forty plus, but I believe they are a commodity and, are outnumbered by the forty plus women. This makes it harder to encounter them. Even the ones I have encountered, although not many, have unique characteristics (another book).

There seems to be a larger, pool of thirty plus men/stallions who are available, secure, financially sound, confident men who encounter forty plus women in their same boat. Most men in this boat, have no baggage like baby mama drama, have not had the life sucked out of them by a horrible marriage and divorce, are on their career paths, and are mature enough to know what they want out of life. If they have experienced marriage and it did not go well, they have learned from the marriage and seek a mellowed, single, lady who compliments them. They move on from undeveloped ways of some younger women and now seek a lady who has a stable and sound persona. They have done the bar, club, and dating the juvenile twenty-something, pretty girls and are looking for an independent, well established, secure, fun and attractive woman to share their lives. How do I know? Again, I keep experiencing it, and know it will keep happening to me. All of the guys I have met recently have been twenty-eight to thirty something. There are some forty plus men, but they are rare. I do not encounter many my age or close to my age in the city where I presently live. Am I looking for someone my own age or younger? No, not necessarily. I am not looking at all. These 30+ men are looking for and finding me, and other ladies like me.

———— ❖ ————

There is Irony in This Book

The reason I write this book is to change societies pessimistic, ideology that believes ladies over forty are pursuing, pouncing and preying on younger men/developing men. Again, we are not all desperate ladies; in fact we are ladies who are taking our time to encounter the gentleman who is right for us, like Loren in the prior story.

On You Tube, on her own website, Beyond Black and White, and having purchased her book four years ago, I follow a woman by the name of Christelyn Karazin, co-author of "Swirling - How to Date, Mate, and Relate. Mixing Race, Culture, and Creed," who speaks to women about the more accepted practice and option we have as women, especially black women, to date other races of men. She has taken a lot of negative comments, hits and threats on all of her sites by those who are opposed to interracial dating. Freely discussing her views on interracial dating, she makes it clear: a woman should always be aware of a man's character before she even thinks about his color. I agree with her.

Age, just as I feel about color, should not make a difference in who you chose to fall in love with. I also agree with her statement of "character before color." She states her motto is derived from the "I Have A Dream" speech by Dr. Martin Luther King, Jr. In it he states, "people should not be judged by the color of their skin, but by the content of their character." Who people are, not what color or age they are, should be the only attribute, which carries weight. Maturity, love, protection, security, and a providing for his family, MARE, or other significant other are the most important characteristics to a lady.

Why am I looking for a developing/younger man? Actually, I am not. Fooled you. I am personally hoping to encounter a mate closer to my age, or not more than ten years. Being able to relate to the same jokes, the same music, the same or similar experiences, being physically appealing, is key for me. Unless the man under forty, is an old soul, and is able to connect with my experiences, then I don't feel we would be compatible. Don't get me wrong. There are developing men out there who have old souls; however, I have not encountered them, yet.

If you know of one, please get in contact with me. I will make a deal with you. If you are successful in finding the right man at a reasonable age for me, and we marry, I promise we will fly you to our wedding, wherever it is. You, my dear, will earn a special place at the head table or receive special recognition. Deal?

———— · ✦ · ————

As a MARE, it is my goal to be the best example I can be. I strive to be mature by the way I handle situations. I work on being attractive inside and out. I act respectable whether I am in public or in private (I even say excuse me to my dogs when I burp. I know, there are special places for people like me) therefore demonstrating respectfulness. Even when provoked in my spirit and body, I fight hard to remain even-tempered, and desire to be know as easy-going, not a drama princess or queen. Finally, I make every effort at being a stable, special sister to my sisters, same gendered women or my close sister-friends.

My mantra is not being the other woman in any relationship. I am too extraordinary, and I know my prince will come, when I'm ready to receive him. I am not claiming by any means to be perfect. I only aim to be what God expects me to be as one of His. It's tough at times, but I find pleasure when others comment on my positive demeanor. I tell them I am a work in progress.

<hr/>

This is not a book on how to. It is merely something for its readers and other to consider as a new group of ladies who want the world to take us seriously. We expect there will be a day when the double standard of the older man-younger woman relationship being normal, to a day when the forty plus ladies and younger/developing men relationship is also readily accepted.

There is a song by Faith, Hope and Charity I heard years ago entitled, "To Each His Own." Even at my young age when my dad would play this song, I knew what it meant.

It should be no one's concern what others are doing or who they are dating, unless it is harmful. I believe there are those who are genuinely interested in the actions of their friends or family who they love. They want to offer another constructive view into a situation in which their friend or family member may become involved. This is healthy and welcomed. Then there comes a time these same people want to judge the person they are offering their opinion or advice. This is when things change and the song; "To Each His Own" is applicable. It's okay to offer an opinion. An open-minded person would listen, and be thankful for someone's perspective. I know I do. When people don't agree with advice they have been given, or don't do what someone has told them, it is okay. People must live their own lives and make their own mistakes, if one is to be made. I have heard so many times and from so many people "experience is the best teacher," but fortunately and unfortunately it is true in most situations. Experience=familiarity=knowledge. M.A.R.E.S. have learned from their experiences. Experiences should teach everyone many different lessons and the wise person should always learns something new from them. I have gained so much wisdom from life. There are things I have encountered and will work hard not to do again, and there are things in the world I will do again because I know how to approach them and get through them.

I know relationships and love have some boundaries, yet are NOT dictated by society and immature people.

M.A.R.E.S are a new group of ladies with different and classier characteristics than the perceived antiquated, negative connotation of a Cougar. There are some who still identify with being a Cougar, and that's okay for them. However, from this point forward, please.... Don't ever call me a Cougar.

EPILOGUE

I attended a film festival in my town. There was an opportunity view a short film of 4:38 minutes entitled, Cougar. I thought, "Oh boy. Here we go again."

At the opening of the short film, a beautiful, forty plus woman is seated at a table, facing the bar. In walks a man who appears to be in his thirties. She spots him. As he sits at the bar waiting for his drink, he scopes out the place. Turning around in his chair, he makes eye contact with the woman. She responds with a head nod. His drink comes and he takes a swallow. He turns once more, casing the establishment, and once again makes eye contact with the woman. She responds by raising her glass. He smiles back and raises his glass in gesture.

Seconds go by, she then writes something on a napkin. It's a ticktacktoe game. She starts with an X and motions for the waiter to take the napkin to the man seated at the bar. The waiter gives the napkin to the gentleman at the bar. He smiles then joins in. He places an O on the napkin, and the waiter takes it back to the woman. She responds to the games with her X AND, her room number. This time she gets up from her table, and delivers the game in person. She pays for their drinks, and then heads to the elevator. He throws his head and his drink back, sets the glass on the bar and follows her.

They are both facing the elevator door. When the elevator door opens, they both get in. No words are spoken. He tries to kiss her, but she eludes his lips, teasing him. He smiles. As the elevator doors open, they both exit and walk to her room. She fumbles in her purse for her room key. She smiles. She turns towards him and allows him to kiss her, gently. He smiles. He knows he is minutes away from a good time.

She turns and finally places the key in door. The audience can feel his anticipation. As she opens the door, she motions for him to enter first. When he steps into the room, he is greeted with, "SURPRISE!"

His friends are waiting in the foreground with a lit cake and birthday decorations. He turns to the COUGAR, and gives her a big smile. In her coolness and having carried out her mission, she turns and walks down the hall.

What was I thinking? What were YOU thinking?

ENDNOTES

[i] Ali, Kecia. 2014. The Lives of Muhammad. Cambridge, Massachusetts: Harvard University Press, 2014. eBook Collection (EBSCOhost), EBSCOhost (accessed October 27, 2016).

[ii] Stewart, Michael. "Siren/Mermaid" quicksilvermint.com.hyyp://www.quicksilvermint.com/medallion/pages/siren.html (accessed Oct. 29, 2016)

[iii] Hitron, Haggai. "Playing Himself to Tears" www.haaretz.com. http://www.haaretz.com/israel-news/culture/leisure/playing-himself-to-tears-1.264390 (accessed October 30, 2016)

[iv] Tessina, Tina. The Unofficial Guide to Dating Again. Hoboken: Wiley, 1999.

APPENDIX

Bet You Didn't Know....

According to a Florida Atlantic University study by Ryne Sherman, Associate Professor of Psychology, Charles E. Schmidt College of Science, "Millennials are the most sexually INACTIVE group since the Great Depression of the 1920's.

Because:

1. There is more sex education.
2. There is a greater awareness of STI/STD'S.
3. They are growing up slower.
4. They have easier access to pornography.
5. They have differing definitions of what sex is. Oral vs. Intercourse.

Millennials are now outnumbering Baby Boomers, and being touted as the "nation's largest living generation." They are defined as those who are 18–34 and statistically are 75.4 million in number. This number is increasing because younger, immigrants are expanding its ranks in the U.S., in addition to the natural, population, growth in the U.S. as a result of Millennials having their own children.

Generation X's are the "middle children." They are between Millennials and Boomers. Considered smaller in number and were born during a period Americans were having less children, Gen Xers range from 35-51 in age. There are about 64 Million of them, however they will surpass the Boomers by 2028.

The Boomers are defined by the growth in U.S. births following World War II. They are older and their numbers shrinking as the number of deaths among them exceeds the number of older immigrants arriving in the country. Boomers, for the record, number 74.9 million and are 51-69 in age.

Richard Fry -Senior Researcher
Pew Research Center- Jan. 16, 2015

What age difference would you accept in your partner?

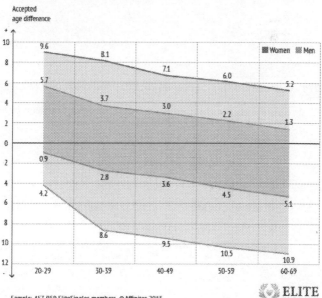

Sample: 453,959 EliteSingles members ©Affinitas 2015

ELITE SINGLES

Generation X: Stuck in the Middle

Gen Xers are the demographic bridge between the predominantly white Baby Boomers and more diverse Millennials. They also fall in the middle on other demographic measures.

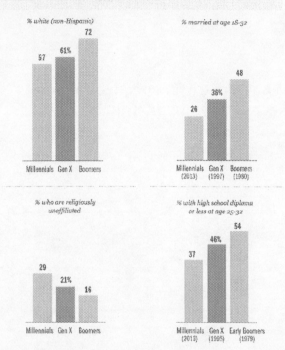

% white (non-Hispanic)

Millennials 57 — Gen X 61% — Boomers 72

% married at age 18-32

Millennials (2013) 26 — Gen X (1997) 36% — Boomers (1980) 48

% who are religiously unaffiliated

Millennials 29 — Gen X 21% — Boomers 16

% with high school diploma or less at age 25-32

Millennials (2013) 37 — Gen X (1995) 46% — Early Boomers (1979) 54

Gen Xers' attitudes on political and social issues often fit between those of the more conservative Baby Boomers and more liberal Millennials.

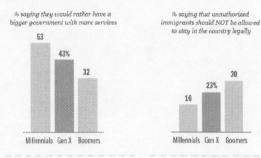

% saying they would rather have a bigger government with more services

Millennials 53 — Gen X 43% — Boomers 32

% saying that unauthorized immigrants should NOT be allowed to stay in the country legally

Millennials 16 — Gen X 23% — Boomers 39

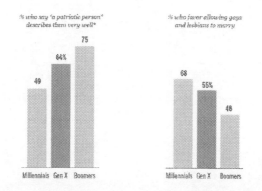

	Millennials	Gen X	Boomers
Patriotic	49	64%	75
Favor gay marriage	68	55%	48

When it comes to technology use and adoption, Generation Xers find themselves again in the middle.

*% saying they have shared a "selfie" on social media***

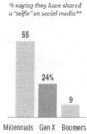

Median number of Facebook friends (among Facebook users)

	Millennials	Gen X	Boomers
Shared a selfie	55	24%	9
Median FB friends	250	200	98

(Ages 49-57 only)

Like their namesake suggests, Gen Xers are less distinct than other generations. And they know it.

% saying their generation is unique (2010)

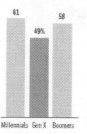

	Millennials	Gen X	Boomers
Generation is unique	61	49%	58

* Percentages reflect those who rated each description 8-10 on a scale of 1-10 where "10" is a perfect description and "1" is totally wrong.

** Respondents who answered "yes" when asked if they knew what a "selfie" was were asked if they had ever shared a selfie on a photo sharing or social networking site such as Facebook, Instagram or Snapchat.

Source: Taylor, Paul. The Next America. Public Affairs Press, 2014 and various Pew Research Center surveys. Data are for 2014 or 2013 unless otherwise noted. Millennials include only their adult population ages 18 and older.

PEW RESEARCH CENTER

BIBLIOGRAPHY

Ali, Kecia. 2014. *The Lives of Muhammad*. Cambridge, Massachusetts: Harvard University Press, 2014. *eBook Collection (EBSCOhost)*, EBSCO*host* (accessed October 27, 2016).

Burrell, Lynette. "Age is Just a Number to Younger Men, Who Now Prefer Dating Older Women" www.medicaldeaily.com. http://www.medicaldaily.com?age-just-number-younger-men-who-now-prefer-dating-older-women-320136 (accessed January 21,2017)

Brings, Felicia and Winter, Susan. Older Women, Younger Men: New Options for Love and Romance Far Hills: New Horizon Press, 2000.

Hitron, Haggai. "Playing Himself to Tears" www.haaretz.com. http://www.haaretz.com/israel-news/culture/leisure/playing-himself-to-tears-1.264390 (accessed October 30, 2016)

Stewart, Michael. "Siren/Mermaid" quicksilvermint.com.hyyp://www.quicksilvermint.com/medallion/pages/siren.html (accessed Oct. 29, 2016)

Taylor, Paul.*The Next America*. Public Affairs
Press, 2014 and various Pew Research Center
surveys

Tessina, Tina. The Unofficial Guide to Dating
Again. Hoboken: Wiley, 1999.

"THANK YOU!"
XOXO

Find Me at: www.meetsherrylynne.com